The American Heritage
SCHOOL DICTIONARY
Activities Book

Dr. TINA THOBURN
*Director, Tintern Research
& Educational Enterprises*

TERRY THOBURN
Educational Writer

HOUGHTON MIFFLIN COMPANY / BOSTON
ATLANTA   DALLAS   GENEVA, ILL.   HOPEWELL, N.J.   PALO ALTO

Copyright © 1972 by Houghton Mifflin Company

All rights reserved. No part of this work may be reproduced or transmitted in any form or by any means, electronic or mechanical, including photocopying and recording, or by any information storage or retrieval system, without permission in writing from the publisher.

PRINTED IN THE U.S.A.

ISBN: 0-395-13851-5

UNIT 1
From A to Z

Open your dictionary to any page. The words in heavy black type that begin a little farther to the left than the rest of the material are called **main entry words.**

The main entries are arranged in alphabetical order. As you know, that means that the words that begin with the letter **a** come first, then those that begin with **b**, and so on, until at the end you will find the words that begin with **z**.

To find a main entry quickly, you need to be very familiar with the order of letters in the alphabet. These exercises will give you a quick review.

1. Fill in the missing capital letters.

A   B   __   __   __   __   __   __   I   __   __   __   __   __

N   __   __   __   __   S   T   __   __   __   __   __   __   Z

2. Fill in the missing lower case (small) letters.

__   __   c   __   __   __   __   h   __   __   __   __   __   __

__   o   __   __   r   __   __   __   __   __   __   x   __   __

3. The alphabet below is scrambled. Below each letter write the number that shows its order in the alphabet.

l	i	s	c	g	p	a	x	e	v	j	y	m
												13
h	o	t	b	k	w	q	z	f	u	n	r	d
		20				17						

Which letter is numbered 16? _____   Which letter is numbered 4? _____

Which letter is numbered 5? _____   Which letter is numbered 24? _____

Which letter is numbered 12? _____   Which letter is numbered 10? _____

From A to Z

4. Which of the two letters in each group below comes nearer the beginning of the alphabet? Underline it.

    a x   Y d   n m   l j   M R   n g   O K   c q   D e   s r

5. Which of the two letters in each group below comes nearer the end of the alphabet? Underline it.

    c m   e h   Q J   l s   f t   K P   i n   q u   n f   v w

6. Which letter in each group below comes between the other two in the alphabet? Underline it.

    S R O   c a b   U H F   V I P   g y m   j e t   n o t   f r y

7. Before each letter below, write the letter that comes just before it in the alphabet. After the letter write the letter that comes just after it.

___ C ___   ___ H ___   ___ T ___

___ s ___   ___ v ___   ___ u ___

___ b ___   ___ N ___   ___ j ___

___ o ___   ___ Q ___   ___ d ___

___ e ___   ___ p ___   ___ L ___

___ Y ___   ___ f ___   ___ x ___

8. The letters and numbers in Exercise 3 make a good code. Use it to unscramble the following riddle.

Under each number, write the letter that comes in that order in the alphabet. Under 1, you would, of course, write a.

Q. 23-8-1-20   9-19   20-8-5   13-15-19-20   9-13-16-15-18-20-1-14-20   21-19-5

6-15-18   3-15-23-8-9-4-5?

A. 8-15-12-4-9-14-7   3-15-23-19   20-15-7-5-20-8-5-18!

Which Quarter?

One way to find a word quickly is to think of the dictionary as being divided into four equal sections, which we will call **quarters**. Each quarter contains about the same number of words as every other quarter. Since there are twenty-six letters in the alphabet, you might expect six or seven of them to fall in each quarter. Dividing the dictionary doesn't work that way, however, because more words are listed under some letters than under others. For example, the letter S begins more words than **I**, **K**, **Q**, **U**, **V**, **W**, **X**, **Y**, and **Z** do together, and **C** begins nearly twice as many words as **D**.

When the dictionary is divided into quarters, it comes out about like this:

The first quarter contains A, B, C, D.
The second quarter contains E, F, G, H, I, J, K, L.
The third quarter contains M, N, O, P, Q, R.
The fourth quarter contains S, T, U, V, W, X, Y, Z.

1. Which letter begins the second quarter? _____

2. Which two letters come just about at the middle? _____ and _____

3. Which letter begins the fourth quarter? _____

4. After each word below, write the word that tells which quarter of the dictionary you would expect to find it. The first answer has been written in for you.

notebook	_Third_	valentine	_____	bride	_____
tambourine	_____	antique	_____	groom	_____
Kayak	_____	porcupine	_____	yak	_____
weasel	_____	dentist	_____	umbrella	_____
handkerchief	_____	saucer	_____	flag	_____
queen	_____	library	_____	zebra	_____
candle	_____	elephant	_____	range	_____

Which Way?

Once you have decided in which quarter of the dictionary the word must be, the next problem is to find the place in that quarter where all the words begin with the same letter as your word.

For example, you are looking up the word *quatrain*, and you first open the dictionary to a page where all the words begin with *s*. You must decide whether to turn toward the front or the back of the book. Because *q* comes before *s* in the alphabet, you must turn toward the front. If you had turned to a page where all the words began with *p*, you would have to turn toward the back of the book, because *q* comes after *p* in the alphabet.

1. Suppose that you are trying to find the word *fortnight*, but you open first to the place where all the words start with the letter *e*. Would you then turn toward the front of your dictionary or toward the back? Why would you turn in that direction?

   I'd turn toward the _____, because *f* comes _____ *e*.

2. If you had turned to a page of words that begin with *h*, which way would you turn to find the word *fortnight*? Why?

   I'd turn toward the _____, because *f* comes _____ *h*.

3. Suppose you are trying to locate each word below, but you open your dictionary to words that begin with the letter in parentheses. In the blank following the parentheses, write *front* or *back* to show which way you would turn to find your word.

   time (s) _____

   calendar (d) _____

   hour (j) _____

   day (c) _____

   nuclear (m) _____

   your (z) _____

   expert (c) _____

   aftermath (b) _____

   lightyear (h) _____

   perennial (q) _____

   century (b) _____

   millennium (o) _____

   biennial (c) _____

   future (e) _____

Look Further

After you have found the words that begin with the same letter as the word you are looking up, your troubles aren't over. You may discover that when you have found the words that begin with *f*, there are over fifty pages of them!

All the words that begin with the same letter are not just lumped together any old way. They are placed in alphabetical order according to the letters that follow the first one. For example, *face* comes before *feel*, because *a* comes before *e* in the alphabet. If the first two letters are the same, the third letter determines which order the words come in. For example, *face* comes before *fade*, because *c* comes before *d* in the alphabet.

1. In each pair of words below, put a check (✓) before the word that would come first in the dictionary. Draw a line under the letter that told you so.

| ___ bread | ___ make | ___ never | ___ pack | ___ quit | ___ miss |
| ___ butter | ___ mail | ___ night | ___ parade | ___ queer | ___ mess |

| ___ sandal | ___ ballet | ___ million | ___ poke | ___ pass | ___ bush |
| ___ saddle | ___ basket | ___ multiply | ___ pocket | ___ posse | ___ brush |

2. Sometimes you must go to the fourth or fifth letter before you find one that is different. In each pair below, check the word that would come first in the dictionary. Draw a line under the letter that told you so.

| ___ mirror | ___ bright | ___ launch | ___ threaten | ___ motion | ___ shock |
| ___ miracle | ___ brick | ___ laundry | ___ thread | ___ motive | ___ shove |

| ___ telegram | ___ mister | ___ moss | ___ distant | ___ whisper | ___ bend |
| ___ telephone | ___ misty | ___ most | ___ distract | ___ whistle | ___ bent |

3. Now that you've had some practice in deciding which word comes first in your dictionary, let's try some groups of three. You may have to go to the fifth, sixth, or seventh letter or even beyond that. In each group below, number the words 1, 2, and 3, according to the order in which they would come in your dictionary.

___ demolish	___ telescope	___ division	___ operate	___ simply
___ demon	___ telephoto	___ divinity	___ operable	___ simplify
___ demolition	___ telephone	___ divisible	___ operation	___ simple

___ multiply	___ particle	___ previous	___ apparel	___ snorkel
___ multiple	___ participate	___ prevent	___ apparition	___ snore
___ multiplication	___ partition	___ preview	___ apparent	___ snort

4. Sometimes you may run out of letters to compare, as with the words *less* and *lessen*. Just remember the shorter word comes first.

Sometimes the same word is written with a small letter and with a capital. The word beginning with the small letter comes first.

In each pair of words below, put a check before the word that would come first.

| ___ poetry | ___ March | ___ rove | ___ creek | ___ bully | ___ sting |
| ___ poet | ___ march | ___ rover | ___ Creek | ___ bull | ___ stinger |

5. In each column below, number the words from 1 through 6 to show the order in which you would expect to find them in your dictionary.

___ mayor	___ derail	___ scourge	___ margarine	___ frankfurter
___ mayflower	___ derive	___ scour	___ march	___ frail
___ May	___ Derby	___ scotch	___ marble	___ frank
___ mayonnaise	___ derailment	___ scorpion	___ March	___ franc
___ may	___ derby	___ scone	___ margin	___ frame
___ mayhem	___ derange	___ Scotch	___ mare	___ Frank

7

Guiding the Way

Find the word *baseball* in your dictionary. Now look at the two words in heavy black type at the very top of the page. They look like this: **barrister|basis**. Notice that the word *barrister* is the first entry on the page and that *basis* is the last entry. Those words are called **guide words**. Every other entry on that page comes between the guide words in alphabetical order.

To find a word in your dictionary, first decide in which quarter of the dictionary the first letter of the word occurs. Second, turn toward the front or back to locate all the words that begin with that letter. Next, use the guide words to find the exact page on which your word occurs.

1. Which words below would occur on a page that has as guide words **grenade** and **gripe**? Put a check before each such word. Before each word that you did not check, write B if it comes before this page and A if it comes after this page.

___ grumble   ___ greyhound   ___ grip   ___ gremlin   ___ griddle

___ griffon   ___ greenwood   ___ groom   ___ grille   ___ grieve

___ grog   ___ grindstone   ___ Grimm   ___ grime   ___ gristle

2. Below are the guide words for three different pages in your dictionary. After each word in the lists below, write I, II, or III to show on which page the word is listed. If the word is not listed on any of those pages, leave the space blank.

I **carpus|Carthage**   II **Cartier|cash**   III **cash crop|castigate**

carriage ___   carry ___   carol ___   carve ___

cashew ___   cascade ___   cardigan ___   caries ___

career ___   carousel ___   caret ___   carrot ___

Carson ___   cassette ___   carpenter ___   cartel ___

carhop ___   cartridge ___   cartoon ___   casein ___

casement ___   carpal ___   casserole ___   casual ___

8

3. Pretend that you are looking up each of the entries listed below. If you turn to a page with the guide words listed after the entry, decide whether the entry will be found on that page. If it will, write *On this page* in the blank following the guide words. If the entry comes before or after this page, write *Before* or *After* in the blank following the entry.

ENTRY	GUIDE WORDS	LOCATION OF ENTRY
cruelty	crown | crusade	_____
gangway	gaiter | gamble	_____
hookah	hooves | horoscope	_____
mandrill	mangy | mannish	_____
prejudice	preen | premiere	_____
register	regiment | rehearsal	_____
slander	slat | sleepy	_____
languid	lament | landslide	_____
majority	maintop | make	_____
elicit	eleven | eloquent	_____
Bible	better | bias	_____
national	nationalize | nauseate	_____
igloo	idler | illicit	_____
disperse	disloyal | dispense	_____
fetish	fermium | fetter	_____
sportive	splurge | spore	_____
tail	tailcoat | talcum	_____
warlock	wane | warrant	_____

Kinds of Entries

Each of the words you have been looking up in your dictionary is a main entry. Not all main entries are single words. Some main entries are **phrases**, such as *chili sauce* and *figure of speech*. These phrases are listed as main entries because the words in each are used together very often, and sometimes the meaning of the phrase is different from the meaning of the two or three words used separately. Such phrases are listed in the dictionary as if each one were just one long word.

Sometimes you will find words used together, but with hyphens between them as *good-natured* and *Jack-in-the box*. Such combinations are called **hyphenated compounds**.

Phrases and hyphenated compounds are listed alphabetically as main entries and are used as guide words.

Find each of the main entries below in your dictionary. In the first space after each try, write P standing for Phrase or HC standing for hyphenated compound. Add hyphens where they belong. Then write the guide words on the page where you found the main entry.

Entry	Kind	Guide Words
crash dive		
dead letter		
cross country		
two faced		
folk dance		
great grandmother		
grade crossing		
cold hearted		
bird of prey		

Other Kinds of Entries

You have learned that not all entries are single words. Word phrases and hyphenated compounds are also entered as main entries.

Two other kinds of entries are found in your dictionary. Abbreviations are listed as main entries. You'll find such abbreviations as **Mr.** and **Mrs.** in their correct alphabetical order. You'll also find some abbreviations which are written without periods following them, such as **cc** and **IQ**. Not all abbreviations are capitalized.

Contractions, such as **isn't** for *is not* and **I've** for *I have* are listed in their correct alphabetical order and each one is followed by the two words that were put together to form the contraction.

Abbreviations and contractions may be used as guide words.

1. Number the words in each of the groups below as 1, 2, 3, and 4 according to how they would come in alphabetical order, the same order in which all entries are listed.

___ cayuse	___ egret	___ movie	___ plywood	___ ice age	___ op. cit.
___ cease-fire	___ eel	___ muddle	___ poach	___ ibid.	___ open air
___ Cb	___ e.g.	___ Mr.	___ p.m.	___ icicle	___ ooze
___ C clef	___ efface	___ MPP	___ plural	___ ibex	___ onyx

2. Find each contraction in your dictionary. Write the entry that is just before the contraction in the blank at the left and the entry just after it in the blank at the right.

_____ it'll _____

_____ shan't _____

_____ aren't _____

_____ don't _____

_____ they've _____

_____ can't _____

Words That Look Alike

In looking through your dictionary, you have probably noticed that some words have small numbers printed after them and up a little higher than the word. These are called **superscript numbers**.

EXAMPLES: **mark**[1]   **angle**[1]   **desert**[1]
            mark[2]   **angle**[2]   **desert**[2]
                                 desert[3]

These words are called **homographs**. *Homo-* is a prefix that means alike, and *-graph* often means *drawn* or *written*. Homographs are two or more words that are spelled exactly the same way, but that have different meanings and sometimes are pronounced differently.

Homographs are listed alphabetically just as other entry words are, and they are arranged in a group according to the superscript numbers.

Below are some entry words. Find each one in your dictionary. Decide whether it is a homograph. If it is, write the other homographs in that group in the blanks at the right. If it is not a homograph, cross out the superscript number. The first one has been done.

chord[1]   *chord*[2]

flash[1]

gin[1]

last[1]

hard[1]

Neptune[1]

bank[1]

read[1]

port[1]

Two for One

Sometimes in the English language, there are two or more spellings for the same word. We call these different spellings *variants*. Most of the time variants are entered separately in your dictionary. However, if there is no difference in the pronunciation and there are no main entries between them in alphabetical order, they are both listed under one entry.

EXAMPLE: **ax** or **axe**

Sometimes one variant spelling is preferred over another. When this happens, the variants are joined by the word *also* instead of *or*.

EXAMPLE: **enthrall**, *also* **enthral**

1. After each word write the variant given in your dictionary.

good-by _____   myna _____

councilor _____   bourn _____

rajah _____   catalog _____

O.K. _____   granny _____

jinriksha _____   epaulet _____

2. Below are some pairs of variants. Locate each pair in your dictionary and then underline the preferred spelling. In the blank following the pair, write the main entry as it appears in your dictionary. The first one is done for you.

<u>epilogue</u>, epilog *epilogue*   debonaire, debonair _____

jeweller, jeweler _____   to-day, today _____

pavane, pavan _____   kebab, kabob _____

cocoanut, coconut _____   mock-up, mockup _____

judgment, judgement _____   tonight, to-night _____

13

Wrap-Up Page

Below are some main entries from your dictionary. First, write the entries in alphabetical order in the first column. In the second column, write *S* if the entry is a simple word, *P* if it is a phrase, *A* if it is an abbreviation, *C* if it is a contraction, *HC* if it is a hyphenated compound, or *H* if it is a homograph.

In the third column, indicate in which quarter of the dictionary the entry is located and in the last column, write the guide words on the same page as the entry.

ENTRIES

you've	evening gown	nerve-racking	arm
calico	skate	we've	he'll
pawn	IOU	Swiss cheese	queasy

Main Entry	Kind	Quarter	Guide Words

UNIT 2
Parts and Pieces

One reason for looking up an unfamiliar word in the dictionary is to find out how to pronounce it. One of the first clues your dictionary gives is to divide the main entry into **syllables**, provided the word has two or more syllables. A one-syllable word cannot be divided.

Locate the entry **flamboyant** in your dictionary. It is divided into syllables and the syllables are separated by small dots, like this: **flam·boy·ant**.

Some words have only one syllable and some have several syllables.

EXAMPLES: **girl** **at·mos·pher·ic**
aim **de·to·na·tion**

Some syllables have only one letter and some have several letters, but every syllable has at least one of the vowels, *a*, *e*, *i*, *o*, *u* or *y*.

EXAMPLES: **splash·ing** **in·tim·i·date**

If a word has two or more syllables, you can say it in pieces, stopping between syllables.

1. Make a list of words that have only one syllable.

_____ _____ _____

_____ _____ _____

2. Locate each of the following entries in your dictionary. On the blank after the entry, write the word as it appears in your dictionary, separating syllables by dots.

pronounce _____

recess _____

early _____

jury _____

bakery _____

parasol _____

excellent _____

recycle _____

opposite _____

recorder _____

Symbols for Sounds

After every entry in your dictionary is the key to the pronunciation. It comes right after the entry and is set off by vertical lines.

EXAMPLE: **gen·er·al** | **jen′** ər el |

As you can see, the pronunciation is not spelled the same way as the entry. All pronunciations are phonetic respellings of the main entries.

In English, as you know, the sound of a word often doesn't tell you how to spell it. You can hear the same sound at the beginning of *cat*, *kitten*, and *chorus*, but the beginning sound is not spelled the same way.

In the phonetic respelling, each of those words would begin with *k*, because *k* is used to stand for that sound, no matter how it is spelled.

Phonetic means "representing the sounds of speech with a set of symbols, each denoting a single sound."

1. Below are the symbols used for some of the consonant sounds. After each one, write a word that begins with that sound. Turn to the inside cover of your dictionary for help.

b _____ f _____ g _____

ch _____ j _____ k _____

d _____ l _____ m _____

f _____ p _____ s _____

g _____ v _____ z _____

2. Say each word below to yourself. Decide which symbol would be used for the first sound of that word in the phonetic respelling. The inside cover of the dictionary can help you.

city _____ gentle _____ church _____ lamb _____

phone _____ cover _____ money _____ King _____

butter _____ powder _____ giggle _____ funny _____

Symbols for Sounds

3. The symbols you used in exercises 1 and 2 were all letters you use in spelling. Two other symbols which you also use in spelling are the th and th symbols.

The th symbol stands for the sound you hear at the beginning of *think* and *thumb* and at the end of *bath* and *both*. The th symbol stands for the sound you hear at the beginning of *this* and *then* and in the middle of *mother* and *weather*.

After each word below, write 1 if the letters th in that word have the sound that th stands for. Write 2 if the sound is the one that th stands for.

throw _____	bother _____	thank _____	growth _____

death _____	healthy _____	myth _____	bathe _____

breathe _____	there _____	brother _____	neither _____

Now check your answers with your dictionary.

4. Another symbol which may seem confusing to you is the hw. If you make a difference in pronouncing *which* and *witch*, you are using the sound that hw stands for when you say *which*, and the sound that w alone stands for when you say *witch*.

Most words that begin with the letters wh begin with the sound hw stands for, but not all such words do. The word *whole*, for example, begins with the same sound as *how*, and *here*, for which the symbol is h.

After each word below, write the symbol that would be used in your dictionary for the beginning sound. Use hw, w, or h.

whether _____	weather _____	whine _____	whirl _____

whose _____	where _____	wind _____	whiskers _____

whip _____	wholesome _____	whom _____	who _____

wisp _____	whence _____	while _____	wonder _____

5. Another symbol which is used in your dictionary is zh. That symbol stands for the sound you hear in the middle of *treasure* and *vision*. It never comes at the beginning of a word and seldom occurs at the end of any word.

Say each word below to yourself. If you hear the sound zh stands for, put a check mark before the word.

_____ treasure	_____ session	_____ mission	_____ fissure

_____ division	_____ measure	_____ decision	_____ future

Check your answers with your dictionary.

Symbols for Vowel Sounds

You probably don't have any trouble deciding on which consonant sound the symbol stands for. The vowels are a different problem. The English language has more vowel sounds than most other languages do, so in phonetic respelling, each of the five vowels must stand for more than one sound. You have probably noticed that the vowels in the pronunciation key have markings over them. These are called **diacritical marks**.

One mark that you will meet often is the short vowel mark, which looks like this: ă. Each of the five vowels has a short sound. You can hear the short sounds of the five vowels in these five words:

bag   beg   big   bog   bug

In the phonetic respelling, they would look like this:

băg   běg   bĭg   bŏg   bŭg

There are also long sounds. The long sounds of a, e, i, and o sound just like the names of the letters, and they are marked like this: ā, ē, ī, ō. You hear them at the ends of these words: **bay**, **me**, **tie**, and **toe**. The phonetic respelling of those words would be: bā, mē, tī, tō.

Two other vowel sounds are the long **oo** sound heard in **boot** and **food** and the short **oo** sound in **good** and **foot**. The phonetic respelling would be:

boo̅t, foo̅d, goŏd, foŏt.

1. For each question below, draw a line under the correct answer. All the answers are given in phonetic spelling. Use what you've learned about the symbols for sounds.

Which of these would you wear on your head?   kŭp   kăp   kāp

Which of these is a large body of water?   līk   lăk   lāk

Which of these does a weather forecast mention?   răn   rān   rěn

Which of these can you ride on?   bāk   bĭk   bēk

Which of these are you supposed to follow?   rēl   roo̅l   rōl

Which of these is used to stop a car?   brāk   brĭk   broŏk

Symbols for Vowel Sounds

2. Besides the long and short sounds, there are other vowel sounds. Sometimes you will see a mark like this: ä. That symbol stands for the sound you hear in **far** and **arm**.

The letters *a, i, o,* and *u* often are marked like this: â, î, ô, û. These vowel sounds usually come just before the sound of *r*.

EXAMPLES: *Wear* is phonetically wâr.
Deer is phonetically dîr.
Horse is phonetically hôrs.
Her is phonetically hûr.

In addition, the symbol ô stands for the sound you hear in **all**, **caught**, and **paw**.

The symbol yo͞o stands for the sounds you hear in the word you.

EXAMPLES: **Cute** is phonetically kyo͞ot.
Few is phonetically fyo͞o.

The symbol ou stands for the vowel sound in *out* and *cow,* and oi for the vowel sound in *oil* and *boy.*

Underline the correct answer to each question below.

1. Which word means the opposite of *peace*?   wûr   wâr   wôr

2. Which word means *did teach*?   to͞ot   tôt   tăt

3. Which word names a *large animal*?   bîr   bûr   bâr

4. Which word means *not cooked*?   rā   rô   rō

5. Which word is the opposite of *girl*?   bou   boi   bo͞o

6. Which word means a *grassy place*?   lōn   lôn   lēn

7. On which of these would you find pigs and cows?   färm   fôrm   fûrm

8. Which of these names a season of the year?   foil   fôl   foul

9. Which of these do you do when you are hungry?   out   ôt   ēt

10. Which of these is a kind of weapon?   spâr   spîr   spôr

11. Which of these is the opposite of *empty*?   foil   foul   fo͞ol

12. Which word is the opposite of *push*?   po͞ol   po͝ol   pôl

13. Which word is the opposite of *warm*?   kôl   kōl   ko͞ol

14. Which of these is a kind of fruit?   pĭch   pēch   păch

15. Which of these words means *half a quart*?   point   pīnt   pănt

About Accent Marks

You know that the main entry is divided into syllables which are separated by small dots. The pronunciation is also divided into syllables, but dots are not used. Here the syllables are separated by a space a little larger than the space between letters.

EXAMPLE: re dun dant | ri **dŭn**′dnt |

When a word has two or more syllables, not all syllables are spoken with the same emphasis or force. One syllable is usually given more stress than the others. Look at the pronunciation of *redundant* above. The middle syllable is printed in heavier type than the others. That same syllable has an accent mark after it. These two things show that this syllable is to be stressed more than the others.

1. Following are some words and their pronunciations. Put an accent mark on the correct syllable in each pronunciation. Check each one with your dictionary before you mark it.

dimity	dĭm ĭ tē	mismanage	mĭs măn ij	biscuit	bĭs kĭt	mystery	mĭs tə rē
pekoe	pē kō	condition	kən dĭsh ən	sachet	să shā	preserve	prĭ zûrv
apathy	ap ə thē	pedigree	pĕd ĭ grē	puffin	pŭf ĭn	various	vâr ē əs

2. In some words, especially of three or more syllables, you will find a second accent mark. However, the syllable it follows is not printed in heavy black letters.

This is called a secondary accent. That just means that the syllable is spoken with less stress than the syllable with the main accent, but with more stress than other syllables in the word.

EXAMPLES: dictionary | **dĭk**′shən ĕr′ē | interrupt | in′tər **rŭpt**′ |

Look up the following words in your dictionary. In the pronunciation after each word, put accent marks where they belong, and draw a line under the syllable that has the main accent. That syllable is printed in heavy type in your dictionary.

intimidate	in tĭm ĭ dāt	ramshackle	răm shăk əl	wallpaper	wôl pā pər
monoplane	mŏn ə plān	shopkeeper	shŏp kē pər	superman	soō pər măn
aftermath	ăf tər măth	ordinary	ôr dn ĕr ē	overcome	ō vər kŭm

One More Symbol

In working with words of more than one syllable, you have probably noticed in the pronunciations one symbol that you have not read about. It looks like an *e* standing on its head, like this: ə. The name of this symbol is the **schwa** (shwä). The schwa stands for a vowel sound that is not very clear. It is just a sound something like *uh* which comes between two consonant sounds, at the beginning of a word, or sometimes at the end. You can hear the schwa sound at the beginning of *about, around, against.*

You can hear it in the last syllables of such words as *pencil, actor, mother,* and *certain,* and at the end of such words as *comma, panda,* and *zinnia.* It never occurs in a syllable that has an accent mark in this dictionary.

It won't cause you any trouble in pronunciation, as you sort of glide over it, but the schwa sound is spelled in so many different ways that it can cause trouble in spelling.

Now that you know so much about figuring out how a word should be pronounced, you can prove how much you know by doing this exercise. After each word, you will find its pronunciation. Under that are three entries. They may be words or phrases. Pronounce the word to yourself and put a check mark before the word or phrase that most nearly rhymes with it.

1. tar·pau·lin | tär pô′lĭn |
   _____ care a pin
   _____ cars all in
   _____ mar a line

2. an·tique | ăn tēk′ |
   _____ manlike
   _____ can peek
   _____ a stick too

3. butte | byo͞ot |
   _____ rut
   _____ nutty
   _____ cute

4. ten sile | ten′ səl |
   _____ pencil
   _____ then smile
   _____ be still

5. tab leau | tăb′ lō |
   _____ made you
   _____ grab Joe
   _____ dab Lou

6. tab·ard | tăb′ərd |
   _____ stab hard
   _____ labored
   _____ jabbered

21

A Matter of Choice

Some main entries have two different correct pronunciations. Some of them have both pronunciations written out in their full length.

EXAMPLE: de·tour | dē′toor or dĭ toor′ |

Others of such main entries have only the first pronunciation written out. The second pronunciations will give only the syllable that is different from the first pronunciation.

EXAMPLE: op·po·site | ŏp′ə zit or -sit |

If the second pronunciation were written out, it would look like this | ŏp′ ə sit |.

Usually, the first pronunciation given is the one you will hear more often, but sometimes which pronunciation you hear and use will depend upon where you live and how the people around you pronounce the word.

1. Below are some words and one pronunciation of each. Use your dictionary to find out whether the pronunciation given is the first or the second. If it is the first, write 1 before the word. If it is the second, write 2 before the word.

___ baobab | bā′ ō băb′ |

___ hostile | hŏs′təl |

___ eon | ē′ən |

___ clapboard | klăb′ərd |

___ jinni | jĭn′ē |

___ dachshund | däks′hoŏnt′ |

___ kiosk | kē ŏsk′ |

___ launder | lôn′dər |

2. Write the second pronunciation of each of the following words in the blank after the word. Write the whole pronunciation. The first one is done for you.

nincompoop *ning′ kəm poop′*

bedstead _____

acclimate _____

lamentable _____

horizontal _____

rodeo _____

frangipani _____

maverick _____

22

Nouns and Verbs

In your study of grammar, you have probably learned about parts of speech, or you may call them word classes. Either of those terms means the names we give to kinds of words because of the way they are used in sentences.

For example, a word is a **noun** when it is used as the name of one or more persons, places, or things. The things may be ideas, deeds, or many other kinds. Some examples are: *beauty*, *mud*, *speech*, and *climate*. Most nouns, but not all, can be made plural, meaning more than one, by adding *s* or *es* or in some other way.

EXAMPLES: **boy**, **boys**   **fox**, **foxes**   **man**, **men**

In the dictionary, right after the pronunciation, is an abbreviation for the part of speech or word class as which the word is used. The abbreviation *n.* means **noun**.

EXAMPLE: **cli·mate** | klī′ mət | *n.*

Another part of speech is **verb**. A verb often, but not always, tells what someone or something does, did, or will do. The abbreviation *v.* means **verb**

EXAMPLES: declare   declared   will declare
           is   was   will be

1. In your dictionary, you will find that many words can be used as nouns or verbs. For each word below, write two short sentences, in one using the word as a noun, and in the other using the same word as a verb. Write *n.* or *v.* at the end of the sentence.

walk _____

_____

dream _____

_____

show _____

_____

Other Parts of Speech

Two other parts of speech that we use often are **adjectives** and **adverbs**. An adjective is used to describe a noun.

EXAMPLES: a **strong** man   an **old** coat   **happy** days

The abbreviation used for an adjective is *adj*. Adjectives can be used for comparing, as in these sentences:

Bob is **lazy**, but Joe is **lazier**. Tim is **laziest** of all.

Adverbs are most often used to answer these questions about verbs: In what way? When? Where? How? How often? Some adverbs are formed by adding the ending *-ly* to adjectives.

EXAMPLES: **weak, weakly**   **selfish, selfishly**

The abbreviation *adv*. stands for adverb.

1. After each sentence below, write the abbreviation that tells what part of speech the word in heavy black letters is used as. Use the abbreviation *n., v., adj.,* or *adv*.

I got a **good** mark on my English paper. _____

We were puzzled by the **appearance** of the mysterious stranger. _____

Jim **kicked** a field goal to win the football game. _____

I cleaned up our yard for my mother **yesterday**. _____

The people in the stands cheered **loudly** for our team. _____

Joe is the **best** player on our baseball team. _____

Has anyone seen my yellow **sweater**? _____

The cake Mother made for my birthday was **delicious**. _____

On Saturday my father and I **painted** the kitchen. _____

The **fastest** way to travel across the country is by jet plane. _____

The winds did extensive **damage** to trees. _____

Other Parts of Speech

2. The four parts of speech you have just read about are the four that are used most often, and the ones you might become confused in using.

Some other parts of speech are: **preposition, conjunction, pronoun,** and **interjection.**

In the following sentence, the word *on* is used as a preposition:

Please leave this book **on** my desk.

A conjunction is a joining word, such as *and* or *but*. *And* is the conjunction in the following sentence:

The rain soon stopped, **and** the sun came out.

Pronouns are the words we use to stand for nouns. *I* stands for the speaker or writer. *You* is the person spoken to. Some other pronouns are *he, she, it, we, they, me, us, him, her* and *them.*

An **interjection** is a word or phrase that is said with an expression of surprise, anger, or any other strong feeling. Some examples are: *Wow! Hey! Oh!*

The parts of speech you have read about in this section are abbreviated as follows:

    conjunction *conj.*
    preposition *prep.*
    pronoun *pron.*
    interjection *interj.*

3. After each word below, write the part of speech as which the word is used. If you can't decide without help, use your dictionary. The first one is done for you.

invitation _*noun*_

pray _____

happily _____

nephew _____

them _____

alas _____

generous _____

absence _____

miserable _____

deserve _____

operation _____

but _____

into _____

gorgeous _____

once _____

and _____

succeed _____

there _____

happiness _____

often _____

hopeful _____

operate _____

Some Look-Alikes

We discussed homographs earlier in this book. You read that homographs are words that are spelled the same way, but that have different meanings. Sometimes they are pronounced the same way, but sometimes they have different pronunciations. Often they are used as different parts of speech.

EXAMPLE: **bow** | bō | n. A weapon that shoots arrows.
bow | bou | v. To bend the head, body, or knee.
bow | bou | n. Front part of a ship.

Each homograph is listed as a main entry.

1. Find the following groups of homographs in your dictionary. After each one, write the pronunciation and the abbreviation that shows the part of speech. Use accents where needed.

slough¹ _____

slough² _____

mark¹ _____

mark² _____

live¹ _____

live² _____

tear¹ _____

tear² _____

content¹ _____

content² _____

incense¹ _____

incense² _____

Paris¹ _____

Paris² _____

buff¹ _____

buff² _____

2. Each line below begins with a pronunciation. Following the pronunciation are two or three homographs. Underline the homograph or homographs that have the pronunciation given at the beginning of the line.

Use your dictionary for help.

lĕd	lead¹	lead²		kŏn′sōl	console¹	console²	
rou	row¹	row²	row³	dĭ zûrt′	desert¹	desert²	desert³
bās	bass¹	bass²		fôr′tā	forte¹	forte²	

26

More Look-Alikes

In working with homographs, you found that each one was listed as a main entry. That is done because the meanings of homographs are quite different from each other.

Some other look-alikes are not quite so easy to find. Many words in English are used as more than one part of speech and some of those words are pronounced differently when the part of speech is different. Below is the entry for the word *rebel* as it is found in your dictionary.

> **re·bel** |rĭ bĕl'| *v.* **re·belled, re·bel·ling. 1.** To refuse loyalty to an established government or ruling authority or to oppose it by force. **2.** To resist or oppose openly any authority based on law, custom, or convention: *The boys rebelled against the tyranny of wearing ties in summer.* —*n.* **reb·el** |rĕb'əl|. A person who rebels or is in rebellion. —*modifier: a rebel attack; the rebel leader.*

The first pronunciation given is used when *rebel* is used as a verb. Almost at the end of the entry you find this: —*n.* **reb·el** |rĕb'əl|. This is the way *rebel* is pronounced when it is used as a noun.

1. To answer each question below, find the word in your dictionary. Then look through the whole entry to find another pronunciation. After each question, write the pronunciation.

1. How is *separate* pronounced when used as an adjective? _____

2. How is *record* pronounced when used as a verb? _____

3. How is *reject* pronounced when used as a noun? _____

4. How is *digest* pronounced when used as a verb? _____

5. How is *exploit* pronounced when used as a noun? _____

6. How is *project* pronounced when used as a verb? _____

7. How is *upset* pronounced when used as a noun? _____

8. How is *progress* pronounced when used as a verb? _____

9. How is *contest* pronounced when used as a verb? _____

10. How is *convict* pronounced when used as a noun? _____

The Sound-Alikes

Did you ever have trouble deciding whether to write *there*, *their*, or *they're*? Spelling English words correctly is never easy, and words like the three we've just mentioned make spelling even harder. Words that sound just alike, but are spelled differently and have different meanings are called **homophones**.

Homo- means "same" and *-phone* means "sound". Therefore, *homophone* means "having the same sound".

English has a great many groups of homophones.

EXAMPLES: **bare** |bâr| and **bear** |bâr|
too |to͞o| and **to** to͞o| and **two** |to͞o|

1. Each word below has one or more homophone partners. The partners are in a separate list at the bottom of the page. After each word, write its homophone or homophones. If you are not sure of the meaning of any word, you can find the definition in your dictionary.

rain _____	sun _____	gate _____
hare _____	pane _____	pare _____
not _____	bow (bou) _____	right _____
scent _____	knight _____	sight _____
tail _____	wood _____	pale _____
might _____	boar _____	weigh _____

Partners:
mite	write	son	pain	gait	knot
would	pail	pair	tale	site	pear
hair	reign	way	night	bore	cent
bough	sent	rite	rein		

Check your answers with your dictionary.

The Sound-Alikes

2. If your word has a homophone partner, your dictionary will tell you. Look at the very end of the entry. Use your dictionary to find homophones for the words below.

morn	leek	foul
karat	jell	pray
hall	gilt	collar
forth	flair	moose
principle	toe	choir

3. Homophones, as you know, have quite different meanings. In each sentence below, cross out the homophone or homophones that do not belong. Be sure your answer makes sense.

   a. The eagle is a bird of (pray, prey).
   b. One (pain, pane) of this window is cracked.
   c. This chair was made during the (rein, rain, reign) of King George I.
   d. Mary Delfino has the leading (role, roll) in our class play.
   e. The committee has chosen the (sight, site) for the new school.
   f. Knights of old often wore coats of (mail, male).
   g. The hungry baby began to (wail, wale) loudly.
   h. Use this knife to (pear, pare, pair) the potatoes.
   i. The fisherman bought a new (sail, sale) for his boat.
   j. Can you guess the (wait, weight) of this package?
   k. The opposite of *strong* is (week, weak).
   l. Can you find a (blue, blew) crayon for me?
   m. Cows moo, but horses (neigh, nay).
   n. Are these books to be (throne, thrown) away?
   o. Hibernating animals come (fourth, forth) in the spring.
   p. Is a (mite, might) an insect or a member of the spider family?

Check your answers for meaning with your dictionary.

Wrap-Up Page

In Unit Two, you have been learning how to use the dictionary to find the right way to pronounce a word which may be new to you, or to find out whether you have been pronouncing a word correctly.

Of course, you have been using the pronunciation key which is in your dictionary, but the skills you have learned will help you to use any dictionary. If the diacritical marks or other items in the key are different from the ones in your dictionary, all you have to do is consult the pronunciation key which is given in every dictionary.

1. Following are some words in heavy black type and after each one is the pronunciation. Below each word are three words or phrases. Underline the one that most nearly rhymes with the word.

1. **an·ti·dote** | ăn′tĭ dōt |

    fancy coat

    fan me not

    mainly root

2. **u·mi·ak** | ōō′mē ăk′ |

    come by track

    room we lack

    look, my back

3. **ki·wi** | kē′wē |

    fly high

    he's shy

    peewee

4. **ca·price** | ke prēs′ |

    map press

    a crease

    the rice

5. **pe·o·ny** | pē′ə nē |

    he's bony

    she and I

    see a knee

6. **ex·ca·vate** | eks′kə vāt′ |

    necks have it

    wrecks a gate

    seeks a bat

2. Look up each word below in your dictionary. Find the homophone or homophones for that word. Write the homophone or homophones on the line after the word.

leak _____

born _____

flea _____

mite _____

steel _____

creak _____

flow _____

tier _____

UNIT 3
What Does It Mean?

Often you read or hear a word the meaning of which you do not know. The dictionary is the place to find out. The explanation of the meaning or meanings is called the **definition**. Sometimes two or more meanings are given for a word. If a word has only one meaning, the definition appears in regular type right after the abbreviation that stands for the part of speech.

dish•tow•el |dĭsh′tou′əl| *n.* A towel for drying dishes.

If a word has two or more meanings, the definitions are numbered, beginning, of course, with 1.

dish•wash•er |dĭsh′wŏsh′ər| *or* |-wô′shər| *n.*
1. A machine that washes dishes. 2. A person hired to wash dishes, especially in a restaurant.

1. To answer each question, look up the definition of the word in heavy black type. Decide on the answer and write it in the blank after the question. The first one is done.

Is an **adversary** a friend or an enemy? _An enemy_

Is **pemmican** food or a kind of weapon? _____

Does a **mendacious** person usually tell the truth or a lie? _____

Is a **kinkajou** a bird or an animal? _____

Which is usually found in a **cruet**, vinegar or ink? _____

Which is a **tiara**, a dance or something to wear? _____

Is a **kayak** a boat or an animal? _____

What would you find in an **aviary**? _____

Does a **ewe** have four legs? _____

If you had a **sitar**, would you play it or eat it? _____

Is a **discus** usually thrown or used on a table? _____

Choosing a Meaning

As you know, some words have two or more definitions which are numbered. When you are looking up the meaning of a word, you must decide which of the definitions will make sense in what you are reading or writing.

In your dictionary, the entry for dishwasher looks like this:

dish·wash·er |dĭsh′wŏsh′ər| *or* |-wô′shər| *n.*
1. A machine that washes dishes. 2. A person hired to wash dishes, especially in a restaurant.

EXAMPLES: We have an electric **dishwasher**. (Meaning 1)
We have a human **dishwasher**; I'm it! (Meaning 2)

1. Look up each word in heavy type in the following sentences. Decide which definition fits the meaning of the sentence, and write the number of that definition in the space after the sentence. The first one is done for you.

A **locust** looks something like a grasshopper. _Meaning 1_

My father planted a **locust** in our yard. _____

Alice likes soap that is scented with **lavender**. _____

Mary is wearing a **lavender** sweater and a purple skirt. _____

The **icy** wind made me shiver. _____

In winter, accidents often occur on **icy** roads. _____

My grandmother had only one **child** who is my father. _____

The lost **child** was crying for his mother. _____

The farmer stored most of his corn in a **crib**. _____

The baby learned how to climb out of his **crib**. _____

Do you know how to play a **recorder**? _____

Mr. Anderson is the **Recorder** of Deeds for the county. _____

More About Homographs

You know that homographs are words that are spelled the same way. Most of the time they are pronounced the same way too. However, the words have different meanings. In your dictionary, homographs have small superscript numbers like this: tag^1.

EXAMPLES: The price **tag** on this is $5.00. (tag^1)
We played **tag** at recess. (tag^2)

Each word that is printed in heavy black letters below is one of a group of homographs. Find each word in the dictionary and decide whether it has the meaning of homograph 1, 2, or 3. Sometimes you may find more than that in a group. After each sentence, write the homograph with the correct superscript number.

1. **Palms** grow only in warm climates. _____
2. The men were fishing for **bass** at the beach. _____
3. There is an old **pine** in our back yard. _____
4. My big brother plays the **bass** drum in the band. _____
5. The **palm** of my hand is itchy. _____
6. When we were at the lake, my father caught a **pike**. _____
7. I had to go to the store for a **sack** of flour. _____
8. **Scrub** pines grew all over the sandy island. _____
9. We drove down the **pike** to Midville. _____
10. I had to **scrub** my hands after working in the garden. _____
11. I'd like to learn how to **pitch** a curve. _____
12. The workmen were spreading **pitch** on the road. _____
13. The gardener is going to **prune** the rosebushes. _____
14. The fisherman was mending his **net**. _____

Parts of Speech

You know that some words may be used as more than one part of speech (or word class). After the pronunciation, the abbreviation of the part of speech is listed: n. for noun, v. for verb, adj. for adjective, and adv. for adverb. All the meanings that belong to that part of speech are listed after the abbreviation. Here are two examples:

> **air·lift** |âr'lĭft'| *n.* A system of transporting troops or supplies by air when surface routes are blocked. —*v.* To transport by air when ground routes are blocked.

> **bind·ing** |bīn'dĭng| *n.* **1.** The cover that holds together the pages of a book. **2.** A strip of tape or fabric sewn over an edge or seam to protect or decorate it. —*adj.* Imposing a firm obligation; obligatory: *a binding agreement*.

1. Read each sentence that follows. Decide what part of speech each word in heavy black type is. Remember a word is a noun when it is used to name one or more persons, places, or things. A word is a verb when it can be changed for the time told or asked about, as in **ask**, **asked**. A word is an adjective when it is used to describe a noun. An adverb answers one of these questions: *When? Where? How?* and *How often?* After the sentence write the part of speech as which the word in heavy type is used. If you need help, use your dictionary.

To reach the police, you should **dial** 244-1212. _____

The letters Q and Z are not found on a telephone **dial**. _____

Can you **balance** a ball on your nose? _____

On a **clear** day, you can see Mount Olney from here. _____

I lost my **balance** and got a bad fall. _____

The weather will **clear** before sunset. _____

When the clouds **break**, the sun will shine through. _____

A **break** in the big dam caused a flood. _____

A sneeze doesn't **always** mean that you are catching cold. _____

2. Following are several words which can be used as different parts of speech. Sometimes the pronunciation is different for the two parts of speech. After each pronunciation, write the abbreviation for the part of speech and one meaning for that pronunciation. Use your dictionary to check both the part of speech and the meaning.

an·nex | an′ĕks | _____

an·nex | ə neks′ | _____

proj·ect | proj′ekt | _____

pro·ject | prə jekt′ | _____

in·sert | in sûrt′ | _____

in·sert | in′sûrt | _____

re·ject | rĭ jĕkt′ | _____

re·ject | rē′jekt | _____

rec·ord | rĕk′ərd | _____

re·cord | rĭ kôrd′ | _____

pro·gress | pro gres′ | _____

prog·ress | prog′rĕs | _____

ob·ject | ŏb′ jĕkt | _____

ob·ject | əb jĕkt′ | _____

con·vict | kən vĭkt′ | _____

con·vict | kŏn′vĭkt | _____

sub·ject | sŭb′jĭkt | _____

sub·ject | səb jĕkt′ | _____

con·test | kŏn′tĕst | _____

con·test | kən test′ | _____

35

More About Homophones

You remember that homophones are words which sound just alike, but have different spellings and different meanings.

EXAMPLE: The leaves had fallen and the trees were **bare**.
A grizzly **bear** would not make a good pet.

The definitions in your dictionary will help you spell correctly words that sound just alike. Check the definition to be sure you have used the homophone that makes sense in the sentence.

In the sentences that follow, you will find two or more homophones in parentheses. Underline the one that is correct in that sentence.

On the lines that follow the sentence, write a sentence of your own in which you use the other homophone. If there are three homophones in the parentheses, write two sentences. Use the dictionary definitions for help.

1. Prince George was the (air, heir) to the throne of Ischia.

2. Would you like to spend a vacation on a tropical (isle, aisle)?

3. Bill and Joe rode (there, their, they're) bikes today.

4. Mr. Brown ordered a (choir, quire) of special paper.

5. We need another (hangar, hanger) in the coat closet.

6. The mother of a fawn is called a (dough, doe).

7. This pail won't hold water because there is a (leek, leak) in it.

8. A beaver has a broad, flat (tale, tail).

About Synonyms

Synonyms are words that have the same or almost the same meaning. The words *error* and *mistake* can be used to mean the same thing.

EXAMPLES: I made an **error** in division.
I made a **mistake** in division.

Two words are synonyms of each other if you can substitute one for the other in a sentence without changing the meaning. Synonyms are found in the definitions of a word. A one-word definition is considered a synonym.

Look at the definition that follows **desirable**.

de·sir·a·ble |dĭ zîr′ə bəl| *adj.* **1.** Of such quality as to be desired; pleasing; fine: *a desirable neighborhood.* **2.** Worth doing; advantageous; advisable: *desirable reform.* —**de·sir′a·bil′i·ty,**

The words *pleasing* and *fine* are both synonyms of *desirable*.

Use your dictionary to find a synonym for each word in heavy black type in the sentences below. Write the synonym in the space after the sentence. Look through the definition to find the one word you could substitute in the sentence without changing its meaning.

1. Many accidents **happen** just after sunset. _____

2. Joe certainly has a lot of **pep**. _____

3. Do you have a **query** about this assignment? _____

4. There was a **partial** eclipse of the moon recently. _____

5. We **rehearsed** our class play about twenty times. _____

6. Joan earned the best mark in **orthography**. _____

7. How did you **obtain** that magazine? _____

8. King Waldo's **realm** was not extremely large. _____

9. My first answer was **incorrect**. _____

Using Synonyms

Sometimes you may have a hard time finding just one word that is a synonym for another word. However, you can find a phrase of two or three words which will give the same meaning. We say that such a phrase is **synonymous** with a word, because it can be used in place of the word.

EXAMPLES: Be careful when you **descend** that ladder.
Be careful when you **come down** that ladder.

The dictionary definition will usually give you either a single word or a phrase synonymous with the word you are looking up.

Rewrite each sentence below, using a synonym or a phrase in place of the word in heavy black type. Be sure that you don't change the meaning of the sentence.

1. The attackers **scaled** the walls of the fort.

2. Some elevators **ascend** very slowly.

3. Tom could not **overtake** Bill in the race.

4. How many words did you **misspell**?

5. Does the sun always **rise** in the east?

6. Get a good **grip** on the rope.

7. Do you consider Louisa a **loquacious** girl?

8. Most eggshells are **fragile**.

9. Ellie has a new **aqua** sweater.

10. The witch's brew was made in a **caldron**.

Making a Choice

Sometimes when you look up a word, you find that it has more than one definition. Then you must make a choice. To do this, substitute each definition for the word in the sentence in which you found it.

EXAMPLE: The chopper landed at the airport.
chop·per | **chop′**ər | n. 1. *Slang* A helicopter. 2. Someone or something that chops.

The **helicopter** landed at the airport.
Someone or something that chops landed at the airport.
This substitution will help you decide which meaning makes sense in the sentence. In the example, meaning 1. gives the correct sense.

1. Look up each underlined word below in your dictionary and decide which meaning fits the sentence. Write the number of the correct meaning in the blank before the sentence.

_____ The artist was proud when he sold his first canvas.

_____ We picked forty kumquats off one tree!

_____ Jack was first in line to apply for the job.

_____ Don wanted to flatten John, but he wasn't strong enough.

_____ Most people consider Goliath a giant next to David.

_____ Alice has a scarab on her charm bracelet.

_____ The lost dog wandered into the diner looking for company.

_____ With its curved narrow streets, Boston seems a labyrinth to some people.

_____ George never puts his shirts back on their hangers.

_____ The farmer used a tractor to pull his plow.

_____ Tom was assigned the duty of cleaning the hall.

_____ The deer bounded over the fence.

A Crossword Puzzle

A crossword puzzle is really a game of synonyms. The clues tell you where the synonym of each clue is to go, such as 2 down or 5 across. A good way to do the puzzle is to look up the word in each clue in your dictionary. In the definition, look for a one-word definition, which, as you know, is a synonym.

On the left below are the clues, and on the right are the answers in alphabetical order to make them easy to find. The answers for 1 down and 2 across are done for you. Use your dictionary to find out where the others belong and write them in. When you have written a word in the right place in the puzzle, cross it off on the list of answers.

CLUES

Across

2. jargon
6. kooky
7. lorry
9. divest
12. kerchief
14. bother
17. flippant
18. tomes
20. lecture
21. educe
23. elegant
24. encircle
25. dally

Down

1. knoll
2. fain
3. feat
4. demean
5. astonish
8. lingerie
10. jab
11. keepsake
13. foster
15. grab
16. fend
19. locale
22. glee

ANSWERS

amaze
books
dawdle
disturb
elicit
excellent
exploit
gibberish
gladly
handkerchief
hill
humble
memento

merriment
poke
rear
resist
saucy
scene
snatch
speech
strip
surround
truck
underwear
zany

2. GIBBERISH
1. HILL

A Helpful Clue

Sometimes you will understand a word or a phrase better if you look up another word or phrase which is closely related to it in meaning. For this reason your dictionary has cross-references. They are listed at the end of the entry. Find them in the two entries that follow.

> **American plan.** A system of hotel management whereby the amount charged a guest per day includes meals as well as room and service. See **European plan.**
>
> **European plan.** A system of hotel management in which the amount charged a guest per day covers only the room and service and does not include meals. See **American plan.**

The definition of American plan will help you understand the meaning of European plan, and the meaning of European plan will help you understand American plan. Cross-references help to make meanings clear.

1. Look up each of the following entries. In the space after the entry, write the word or phrase the cross-reference directs you to look up for more information.

flytrap _____

jetsam _____

battery _____

Book of Mormon _____

diatonic scale _____

Gomorrah _____

nova _____

Charybdis _____

Another Clue

Often as you read through the definition of an entry, you will find a phrase or a sentence printed in italics (slanted letters). Such a phrase or sentence is called illustrative, because it illustrates or shows just how the entry is used in our language. An **illustrative** phrase or sentence will be found after the particular definition it illustrates.

else·where |ĕls′hwâr′| *or* |-wâr′| *adv.* Somewhere or anywhere else: *He decided to go elsewhere.*

1. Find each of the words below in your dictionary. Read the definition and illustrative word or phrase, if there is one. Then write an illustrative sentence of your own. Try to make it a sentence that would help someone just learning to speak English.

leathery _____

icing _____

kindling _____

delude _____

jackpot _____

smog _____

Wrap-Up Page

In Unit 3, you have been finding out all the things that the dictionary definition can tell you about a word.

The definition tells you what part or parts of speech the word can be. It gives you at least one meaning for each part of speech. It often supplies an illustrative sentence or phrase, or maybe more than one to show you just how the word is used in spoken and written language.

Following is the entry for the word *sprinkle*.

> **sprin·kle** |spring′kəl| *v.* **sprin·kled, sprin·kling.**
> **1.** To scatter or release in drops or small particles: *sprinkle salt on the icy steps.* **2.** To scatter drops or particles upon: *sprinkle the lawn.* **3.** To rain or fall in small or infrequent drops. —*n.*
> **1.** A small amount; a sprinkling. **2.** A light rainfall; a drizzle.

1. Using the definition for help, answer the questions or follow the instructions given below.

   a. As what parts of speech can *sprinkle* be used? _____

   b. Write the name of each part of speech and after it, write the number of meanings given for it: _____

   c. What illustrative phrases are used in the definition?
   _____
   _____

2. On the lines that follow, write an illustrative sentence for each part of speech as which the word *sprinkle* can be used. At the end of the sentence, write the word that tells the part of speech. Enclose it in parentheses.

   _____
   _____
   _____
   _____
   _____

UNIT 4
Changes of Form

You know that a word is a noun when it is used to name one or more persons, places or things. When a noun names just one, it is a **singular noun**.

EXAMPLES: book, town, idea

If a noun names more than one it is a **plural noun**.

EXAMPLES: books, towns, ideas

Usually the plural noun is formed by adding -s, or -es to the singular noun.

EXAMPLES: bag, bags; box, boxes

If the plural of a singular noun is formed by adding -s or -es to the singular form without any change in spelling, the plural will not be found in your dictionary as a rule. If the plural has a special use or meaning, it will be included.

The plural forms of nouns are called **inflected forms**.

1. Each word below can be used as a singular noun. After each one, write its plural form. Say the singular and plural forms to yourself. If the plural form has the same number of syllables as the singular form, add -s. If the plural has one or more syllable than the singular form, add -es, unless the word already ends in the letter e, as in *slice, slices*.

comb _____	sentence _____	chance _____
number _____	suitcase _____	beach _____
table _____	watch _____	cottage _____
jacket _____	church _____	toothbrush _____
fox _____	crash _____	sneeze _____
syllable _____	page _____	ceiling _____
shirt _____	glass _____	village _____
garage _____	spice _____	peach _____
ditch _____	tax _____	witch _____
ledge _____	price _____	lunch _____
fence _____	shoe _____	ghost _____

Inflected Noun Forms

While just adding -s or -es to most singular nouns will make the plural forms, other nouns change spelling before the ending is added. Words that end with the letter *y* are especially tricky.

EXAMPLES: monkey, monkeys; penny, pennies

Which word changed spelling before -es was added? Look again at *monkey* and *penny*. In *monkey*, the letter before *y* is a vowel, the letter *e*. In *penny*, the letter before the *y* is a consonant; the *y* is changed to *i* before -es is added. You will find the plural of *penny* in your dictionary, because the spelling changes to form the plural. You will not find the plural of *monkey*, because there is no change in spelling.

Some, but not all, nouns that end in *f* or *fe* change spelling to form the plural.

EXAMPLES: leaf, leaves; knife, knives; chief, chiefs

If the *f* in such a word changes to *v* to form the plural, you will find the plural given in your dictionary.

1. After each singular noun form below, write the plural form. Use your dictionary for help if you need it. Put a check mark after each plural given in the dictionary.

lady _____   thief _____   guy _____

roof _____   country _____   enemy _____

life _____   toy _____   loaf _____

key _____   wolf _____   chimney _____

2. Some nouns form plurals in irregular ways. Such plurals are always given in your dictionary. Write the plural form of each singular noun below. Use your dictionary.

man _____   goose _____   mouse _____

sheep _____   ox _____   deer _____

Inflected Verb Forms

You know that a singular noun can be inflected to make the plural by adding -s or -es. Sometimes the spelling of the singular noun is changed when the ending is added.

Verbs are also inflected, usually to show a change in time, but the endings -s and -es are added when the verb is used with a singular noun or with one of these pronouns: *he*, *she*, *it*.

EXAMPLES: Boys shout. A boy shouts. He shouts.

Regular verbs are inflected to show a change in time by the addition of -d or -ed. Adding one of those endings to the **present form,** the form used after the word *to*, changes it to the **past form.**

EXAMPLES: To walk. We walked yesterday.
To sneeze. I sneezed four times.

The form to which endings are added is called the **root word.** If a verb is inflected regularly, and there is no change in the spelling of the root word, only the root word is found in your dictionary.

1. What root word would you look up to find the meaning of each inflected form below?

dissented _____

delighted _____

bewitches _____

exempted _____

cheered _____

impeaches _____

relished _____

exhausted _____

splintered _____

hollowed _____

2. If the present form of a verb ends in the letter *e*, usually only -s or -d is added to the root word. After each inflected form below, write the root word.

pasted _____

encourages _____

operated _____

challenged _____

spliced _____

received _____

More About Inflections

Another way of inflecting verbs is to add the ending *-ing*.

EXAMPLES: walk, walking; read, reading

The *-ing* form of a verb is called the **present participle.** It is used with such helping verbs as *is*, *are*, *was*, *were*.

In inflecting verbs that end in *y*, follow the rule for inflecting nouns that end in *y*. If the letter before *y* is a vowel, simply add *-s* or *-d*. If the letter before *y* is a consonant, the *y* is changed to *i* before *-es* or *-ed* is added.

EXAMPLES: play, plays, played
carry, carries, carried

The *y* is kept before the ending *-ing* is added. If the root word ends with the letter *e*, the *e* is dropped before *-ing* is added.

EXAMPLES: try, tried, trying
change, changed, changing

Remember, if the spelling of the root word changes in any way, the inflected form is given in your dictionary.

1. Complete the table below without using your dictionary.

ROOT WORD	+ -ed	+ -ing	+ -s or + -es
dally			
jounce			
care			
stay			
marry			
hope			

Now check your answers with your dictionary.

More About Inflections

2. Other words that change in spelling when an inflective ending is added are one-syllable words which end with one consonant, and have a short vowel sound as in *hop, hopped, hopping*. Notice that *hope* is inflected like this: *hope, hoped, hoping*. After each root word below, write the word with *-ed* and *-ing* added.

flip _____

grab _____

skid _____

pin _____

whine _____

slap _____

3. If a word of two or more syllables has the accent on the last syllable, and if that syllable ends with a single consonant with a short vowel sound just before it, the final consonant is doubled, as in *omit, omitted, omitting*. If the word ends with the ûr sound, the final *r* is doubled, as in *refer, referred, referring*. After each root below, write the *-ed* and *-ing* forms of that word. Check with your dictionary.

rebel _____

deter _____

admit _____

expel _____

4. In regular verbs, the *-d* or *-ed* form is used as the past tense and as the **past participle**. The past participle is the form used with *have, has,* or *had*. In irregular verbs, the past and past participle are usually different. Under each word below, write the past and past participle. Use your dictionary to be sure you're right.

come   eat   do   freeze

_____   _____   _____   _____

_____   _____   _____   _____

drive   run   ride   give

_____   _____   _____   _____

_____   _____   _____   _____

49

Inflecting Adjectives

You know that a word is an adjective when it is used to describe a noun. Adjectives are inflected when they are used for comparing people, places, or things.

EXAMPLES: happy, happier, happiest
slow, slower, slowest
large, larger, largest
big, bigger, biggest

Regular adjectives can take the -er and -est endings. When -er is added, the word so formed is called the **comparative,** and when -est is added, the word is called he **superlative.**

Sometimes the root word must be changed before either of these endings is added. The rules for adding -er and -est are the same rules as used in adding -ed to verbs.

1. Complete the table below without using your dictionary.

Root Word	Comparative	Superlative
green		
jolly		
fat		
dainty		
clear		
fast		
simple		
handsome		

Now check your answers with your dictionary.

Making Comparisons

You will find the inflected forms of most adjectives in your dictionary. However, the comparatives and superlatives of some adjectives are not formed by adding *-er* and *-est* to the root word. They are formed by using the word *more* or the word *most* before the adjective.

EXAMPLES: Brand X is a *popular* toothpaste.
George is *more popular* than Fred.
Miss Jackson is the *most popular* teacher here.

If no inflected forms are given for an adjective, use *more* and *most* to form the comparative and superlative.

A few adverbs are inflected, such as *soon*, *sooner*, *soonest*. However, most adverbs form the comparative and superlative by the addition of *more* and *most*.

1. Give the comparative and superlative of each adjective in the chart below. Use your dictionary if you need help, but you can probably decide on the right form without help.

Root Word	Comparative	Superlative
silent		
grim		
frowzy		
beautiful		
delicate		
pale		
erudite		

2. Give the comparative and superlative of each adverb.

early _____

fast _____

gladly _____

Adding Suffixes

Besides the inflective endings which you have been learning about, other endings can be added to root words. These other endings make **derived forms.** Usually the derived form is a different part of speech from the root word.

EXAMPLES: govern (verb) + -ment = government (noun)
rapid (adjective) + -ly = rapidly (adverb)
happy (adjective) + ness = happiness (noun)

Endings added to root words are called **suffixes,** and there are many suffixes used in the English language.

1. The suffix *-ment* is often added to a verb to make a noun. After each verb below, write the derivative noun which is made by adding the suffix *-ment*.

enjoy _____

align _____

require _____

engage _____

adjust _____

excite _____

2. The suffix *-ful* is often added to a noun to make an adjective. After each noun below, write the derivative adjective which is made by adding the suffix *-ful*.

cheer _____

color _____

hope _____

grace _____

thought _____

waste _____

3. The suffix *-ly* is often added to an adjective to form an adverb that tells in what way. After each adjective below, write the adverb made by adding *-ly*.

quiet _____

proud _____

pleasant _____

brave _____

cautious _____

rough _____

Using Suffixes

4. In the exercises you have been doing, it has not been necessary to change the spelling of the root word before the suffix is added. However, when the root word ends in *y* with a consonant just before it, the *y* is changed to *i* before the suffix is added to the root.

After each word below, write the derivative that is made by adding the suffix which follows the + sign. Check your answers with your dictionary.

merry + ment = _____

plenty + ful = _____

busy + -ly = _____

beauty + -ful = _____

happy + -ly = _____

fancy + -ful = _____

5. Words that end with silent *e*, such as *fame* and *reverse*, usually drop the *e* when a suffix that begins with a vowel is added. Some suffixes that begin with vowels are *-ous*, *-al*, *-able*. After each root word below, write the derivative made by adding the suffix.

fame + -ous = _____

reverse + -al = _____

love + -able = _____

universe + -al = _____

note + able = _____

ridicule + ous = _____

6. Sometimes two or more suffixes may be added to a word.
Example: accident + -al = accidental
           accidental + -ly = accidentally

Write each word that is made by adding the suffixes to the root words below. You should write two derivatives for each root word. The first one is done for you.

cheer + -ful = *cheerful*

incident + al = _____

care + -less = _____

govern + -ment = _____

play + -ful = _____

beauty + -ful = _____

delight + ful = _____

+ -ly = *cheerfully*

+ -ly = _____

+ -ness = _____

+ -al = _____

+ -ness = _____

+ -ly = _____

+ -ly = _____

53

Finding Derivatives

There are two places in which to look for a derivative in your dictionary. If the spelling, pronunciation, and basic meaning of the root word do not change, derived forms will be found in heavy type at the end of the entry for the root word. The part of speech for each derivative will also be given there.

EXAMPLE:

> **cheer·ful** |chĭr′fəl| *adj.* **1.** In good spirits; happy; gay: *He was cheerful at breakfast.* **2.** Producing a feeling of cheer; pleasant and bright: *a cozy, cheerful room.* **3.** Willing; good-humored: *his cheerful acceptance of responsibility.* —**cheer′·ful·ly** *adv.* —**cheer′ful·ness** *n.*

If the spelling, pronunciation, or meaning of the root word changes, the derived form is sure to be listed in a separate entry.

1. Look up each of these derived forms in your dictionary. Write *S* in the blank if it is listed separately. Write *R* if it is listed in the entry for the root word.

_____ abominable   _____ disappointment   _____ obviously

_____ hoarsely   _____ Oriental   _____ liberalize

_____ occupational   _____ actor   _____ governor

_____ creatively   _____ craziness   _____ demonstration

2. Some of the words below are inflected forms, but others are derived forms. Remember, an inflected form is the plural of a noun, the past, present participle (the *-ing* form), or the past participle of a verb, or the comparative or superlative of an adjective.

Don't let the *-er* ending fool you. If it is used with an adjective, as in *lively*; *livelier*, it is an inflected form. If it is used with a verb to mean the person or thing that does something, it makes a derived form, as *run*, *runner*.

If the word is an inflected form, write *I* before it. Write *D* if it is a derived form.

_____ dancer   _____ sillier   _____ beautiful

_____ dramatist   _____ greediness   _____ gradually

_____ national   _____ hopefully   _____ giggled

Using Prefixes

A suffix, as you know, is an ending attached to a root word. Root words can also have **prefixes,** which are syllables placed at the beginnings of words. A root word plus a prefix is a derived form. A prefix usually changes the meaning of a word, sometimes making it mean just the opposite of its original meaning.

EXAMPLES: happy, unhappy; possible, impossible
read, reread; spell, misspell

The roots about which we have been reading are all words in English, but sometimes you will find prefixes attached to roots which are not words by themselves.

EXAMPLES: expel, propel, repel
In these examples, the root -*pel* has the meaning of *drive* or push.

Prefixes and suffixes are listed as main entries.

EXAMPLES: Prefixes: **ex- re- im- mis-**
Suffixes: **-ness, -ful, -ly, -able**

Where is the hyphen placed in a prefix? Where is it placed in the suffix?

1. Following are some entries that you would find in your dictionary. If the entry is a prefix, write *P* before it. If the entry is a suffix, write *S* before it.

____ bio-	____ -ist	____ -ous	____ -able	____ inter-
____ ante-	____ -ance	____ com-	____ pre-	____ pro-
____ im-	____ -or	____ -ive	____ mis-	____ -ant
____ dis-	____ co-	____ de-	____ fore-	____ -ish
____ -ile	____ -ose	____ be-	____ -ary	____ avi-
____ circum-	____ -ful	____ fore-	____ non-	____ intra-

Prefixes and Meanings

Prefixes are listed as main entries and the meaning of each one is listed.

EXAMPLE:

> **circum–.** A prefix meaning "around, on all sides": **circumnavigate.**

If the prefix has more than one meaning, its meanings are listed and numbered, just as the meanings of words are.

EXAMPLE:

> **re–.** A prefix meaning: **1.** Again; anew: **re-assemble. 2.** Back; backward: **recall.** When *re-* is followed by *e*, it may appear with a hyphen: **re-entry; reentry.**

1. Write the meanings of each of the following prefixes. Then write the word made by adding that prefix to the root after the + sign. Find the meaning of that word and copy it.

a. mid-_____

mid- + day = _____

mid- + stream = _____

b. circum-_____

circum- + navigate = _____

circum + ference = _____

c. co-_____

co- + exist = _____

co- + here = _____

d. bi-_____

bi- + ped = _____

bi- + weekly = _____

Prefixes and meanings

2. After each prefix listed below, write the meanings given for that prefix.
   Then read the sentences which follow the prefix. Decide which meaning the prefix has in the word printed in heavy type. After the sentence, write the number of that meaning.

a. ex- 1. _____ 2. _____

Children under twelve are **excluded** from this swimming pool. _____

My mother is an **ex-teacher**. _____

b. in- 1. _____ 2. _____

You must **insert** the key in the lock to open the door. _____

My assignment is **incomplete**. _____

c. re- 1. _____ 2. _____

I must **rewrite** this letter before I mail it. _____

Did you **return** the book to the library? _____

d. auto-[1] _____ auto-[2] _____

I have **autographs** of some very famous ballplayers. _____

An **automobile** runs under its own power. _____

e. inter- 1. _____ 2. _____

Goods shipped from one state to another are **interstate** shipments. _____

The girls **intertwined** the daisies to make a daisy chain. _____

f. de- 1. _____ 2. _____ 3. _____

The population of this town has **declined** this year. _____

The Arctic flyer had to **de-ice** the wings of his plane. _____

Who can **decipher** this message? _____

What Is An Idiom?

Sometimes we use two or more words together and come up with a meaning that is different from the meanings the words have when used separately. For instance, you know what the word *look* means and what the word *out* means. When you put them together and yell, "Look out!" at someone, you really mean, "Beware!"

Such special groups of words are called **idiomatic phrases** or **idioms**. If a word is used in an idiom, you will find the idiom listed at the end of the definition of the most important word, or key word.

EXAMPLE:

> **bat³** |băt| *v.* **bat·ted, bat·ting.** To move with a flapping motion; blink: *She batted her eyelashes at him flirtatiously.* [SEE NOTE]
> *Idiom.* **bat an eye.** To show surprise: *Jim didn't bat an eye at her answer.*

After each idiom you will find a definition or maybe more than one definition.

1. Underline the key word in each of the following idioms. Then look in your dictionary for the meaning of the idiom. You may find that you picked the wrong key word, so try another word in the idiom. Then write the meaning of the idiom.

for keeps _____

rest on one's laurels _____

on an even keel _____

at a loss _____

not hold a candle to _____

pick holes in _____

make believe _____

down on his luck _____

pave the way _____

Phrasal Verbs

A **phrasal verb** is another kind of idiomatic phrase. A phrasal verb is a verb phrase whose first word is the main-entry word used as a verb. As with idioms, the meaning of a phrasal verb is different from its separate parts. Phrasal verbs are found with their definitions at the ends of definitions of main entries used as verbs.

The first word of a phrasal verb is the key word.

1. Underline the key word in each of these phrasal verbs. Then look up each one and find the meaning. Write the meaning, using your own words if you wish.

follow up _____

cool off _____

rack up _____

pay back _____

mow down _____

point out _____

mark down 1. _____

2. _____

smoke out _____

own up _____

let down 1. _____

2. _____

mix up _____

curl up _____

reel off _____

end up _____

Two Kinds of Modifiers

Adjectives are used to *modify* nouns. An adjective doesn't change the meaning of the noun it modifies, but it adds to the meaning. Whether you say *a tall boy* or *a short boy*, the word *boy* still means the same, but the adjectives *tall* and *short* tell you more about the boy.

Sometimes nouns are used to modify other nouns. For instance, you might talk about a science book. That is just a short way of saying *a book that teaches about science*. An adjective can be compared, and you can use the word *very* before it.

EXAMPLES: This is a new book.
This book is newer.
This book is very new.

When a noun is used as a modifier, you can't compare it or use *very* before it. You can't say, "This book is *very* science." If a noun is used as a modifier, you will find the word *modifier* toward the end of its definition and some examples of how it is used.

1. In each phrase below, the first word is either a noun modifier or an adjective. If it is a noun modifier, write *NM* before the phrase. If it is an adjective, write *A*.

____ lecture hall	____ radio station	____ library card
____ cold winds	____ flat tire	____ horror story
____ poultry farm	____ juicy berries	____ grape jelly
____ happy day	____ moon rocks	____ good movie
____ distress call	____ ranch hand	____ wild country
____ silly idea	____ brave girl	____ busy people
____ orange juice	____ bottle cap	____ rose garden
____ elm tree	____ old jokes	____ tomato plant
____ beaver skins	____ smart trick	____ ice cubes

Wrap-Up Pages

In this unit you have been learning about how words are built up from root words. Before you start doing this page, think back over what you have found out about inflections, derivatives, suffixes and prefixes. If you need to, turn back to the first part of this unit and review these first pages quickly.

1. After each word that follows are four spaces. The first is labeled *Prefix*, the next *Root Word*, and the last two are labeled *Suffix*. Decide whether the word has a prefix, what the root word is, and what suffix or suffixes are used. If there is no prefix or suffix, write *x* in the spaces with those labels. The first one is done for you.

	Prefix	Root word	Suffix	Suffix
a. Unusually	un	usual	ly	x
b. accidentally				
c. misspelling				
d. mournfully				
e. undoubtedly				
f. gracefully				
g. punishment				
h. unkindness				
i. carelessly				
j. reusable				

2. In blank before each word, write *D* if the word is a derivative; write *I* if it is an inflective form.

_____ meaning _____ knocked _____ calmly _____ given

_____ arrangement _____ whipping _____ remarkable _____ laughed

_____ changeable _____ prettier _____ longest _____ amazement

Go on to the next page.

Wrap-Up Pages

3. Find an idiom listed under each of the following words. Use the idiom in a sentence of your own.

best _____

kindly _____

negative _____

please _____

strike _____

rule _____

4. Find in your dictionary how each of the following nouns may be used as a modifier. Write a sentence, using the word to modify another noun.

fir _____

ranch _____

hobby _____

china _____

pirate _____

nylon _____

5. For each entry that follows, find a phrasal verb and use it in a sentence.

buckle _____

hit _____

stay _____

call _____

pin _____

fill _____

UNIT 5
Finding Spellings

Finding a word which you already know how to spell is probably easy for you, but what do you do when you want to find out how to spell a word that you are uncertain about?

The first thing to do is find the words that begin with the letter that stands for the first sound in that word.

Some beginning sounds are always spelled in the same way, but some have two or three different spellings.

1. The following consonant sounds are some of those used in the pronunciation key in your dictionary. When they are used at the beginnings of words, they are always spelled the same way. After each sound and its spelling given here, write three words that you would find under that spelling. Remember, think about the *sound*.

Sound	Spelling	Examples
b	b	
d	d	
hw	wh	
m	m	
p	p	
th	th	
th	th	
v	v	
w	w	
y	y	

2. The l sound at the beginning of a word is almost always spelled with one l, as in *large*. There is one word in your dictionary that begins with ll.

Write the word that begins with *ll*. _____

Write three words that begin with *l*. _____

Beginning Consonant Sounds

Some consonant sounds have two or more spellings. The *k* sound that you hear in *cat* and *kitten* is one of them. It may be spelled *c*, *k*, and *ch*. If it comes just before the *w* sound as in *quick* and *quiet*, it is spelled *q*.

If the sound that comes right after the *k* sound is one of the sounds of *e* or *i*, the beginning k sound is spelled with *k* most of the time, though in a few words it is spelled *ch*, as *chemist*.

If the sound right after the *k* sound is one of the sounds of *a*, *o*, or *u*, the *k* is most likely to be spelled *c*, but occasionally it is spelled *ch*. It is also spelled *k* before a, o, and u sounds.

Before the w sound it is usually spelled *q*.

1. When looking up a word that begins with the *k* sound, think of the sound that comes after it. If the sound is an *e* or an *i* sound, look under *k* first. Then, if you don't find it, look under *ch*.

If the sound right after *k* is a sound of *a*, *o*, or *u*, first look under *c*. If you don't find it, look under *k* and *ch*.

Each word below begins with the *k* sound, but the spelling is not given for the beginning sound. Find the word in your dictionary and write it on the line.

_____ angaroo _____

_____ indling _____

_____ emistry _____

_____ uart _____

_____ atastrophe _____

_____ aos _____

_____ umquat _____

_____ orus _____

_____ ompany _____

_____ oala _____

_____ ettle _____

_____ ourse _____

_____ idnap _____

_____ urrent _____

2. In your dictionary find a word in which the beginning k sound is spelled kh. Write it here.

_____

Beginning Consonant Sounds

3. Another sound that may have more than one spelling is the *j* sound which you hear at the beginning of *joke* and *ginger*.

   If the sound right after the *j* sound is one of the *a*, *o*, or *u* sounds, it is most likely to be spelled *j*. If the sound is one of the *e* or *i* sounds, it may be spelled either *j* or *g*. If you don't find it in one place, look in the other. The letter *g* must always be followed by *e*, *i* or *y* to have the *j* sound in American spelling. In England, our word *jail* is spelled *gaol*.

   Each word below begins with the *j* sound. Find which way the word is spelled and write it.

   _____ ustice _____

   _____ etsam _____

   _____ entlemen _____

   _____ aguar _____

   _____ eneral _____

   _____ elly _____

   _____ enerous _____

   _____ ewel _____

   _____ erbil _____

   _____ erk _____

   _____ igsaw _____

   _____ iraffe _____

   _____ ingle _____

   _____ ymnast _____

   _____ iant _____

   _____ ittery _____

4. The sound that you hear at the beginning of *go* and of *get* is always spelled *g*, but in some words the *g* is followed by *h* or by *u*. In your dictionary, find two words that begin with the letters *gh* and two that begin with the letters *gu*. Write them on the lines below.

   _____

   _____

5. Most words that begin with the sound of *f* also are spelled with the letter *f*, but a few are spelled with *ph* standing for the *f* sound. Below are some groups of three letters. Using your dictionary, find a word that begins with each group of three letters and write it.

   pha _____   phe _____

   phi _____   pho _____

   phr _____   phy _____

65

More About Beginnings

You have learned that some beginning sounds may have alternate spellings. When you are trying to find such words, start looking under the normal spelling for that sound, and if you can't find it, look under an alternate spelling.

Be sure to look for words that sound alike, so that you have the right spelling for the meaning you need.

1. Words that begin with the sound of *n*, such as *never* and *nickel*, most often begin with the letter *n*. However, that beginning sound is sometimes spelled *kn*, or *gn*, or *pn*.

Using your dictionary, find and write three words that begin with *kn*, three that begin with *gn* and two beginning with *pn*. Then write four words that begin with *n*.

_____

_____

_____

_____

2. Under which spelling did you find the most words, *gn*, *kn*, or *pn*? _____

3. The *s* sound is another beginning sound that has alternate spellings. It is sometimes spelled *c* and sometimes *sc*, or *ps*.

If the sound that follows the *s* sound is one of the *a*, *o*, or *u* sounds, the word is most likely to begin with the letter *s*. If the vowel sound after the *s* is one of the *e* or *i* sounds, it may be spelled *c* or *sc*. In American spelling, the letter *c* is followed by *e*, *i*, or *y* if it stands for the *s* sound.

Each word below begins with the *s* sound. Find the correct spelling and write it.

_____ ientific _____   _____ olace _____

_____ ivilian _____   _____ entury _____

_____ ychology _____   _____ yclone _____

4. What two other words are homophones of *sent*? _____

5. The beginning sound of *r* is usually spelled *r*, but in many words the letters *wr* are used as in *wrong*. In some words that begin with the letter *r*, the second letter is *h*. When looking up words that begin with the *r* sound, notice the homonyms that are given so you'll have the right spelling for your meaning.

On the lines below, write three words that begin with *wr*, and three beginning with *rh*.

_____

_____

What homophones are given for the word *write*? _____

6. The *sh* sound at the beginning of a word is almost always spelled *sh*. It is spelled *s* in the words *sure* and *sugar* and their derivatives.

It is spelled *ch* in a few words which we have adopted from the French. *Chauffeur* is one of them.

The letters *ch* at the beginning of a word usually stand for the sound at the beginning of *chair*, but you know *ch* can sometimes stand for the *k* sound. After each word below, write what the *ch* stands for, *sh*, *ch*, or *k*.

chattel _____   chassis _____   chateau _____   character _____

chatelaine _____   choir _____   chignon _____   chicanery _____

chorus _____   chortle _____   chimera _____   chestnut _____

chauffeur _____   chemistry _____   chalice _____   christen _____

chiffon _____   chieftain _____   chrome _____   chapeau _____

chrysanthemum _____   chowder _____   charm _____   chasm _____

7. The *z* sound that you hear at the beginning of *zoo* and *zebra* is most often spelled *z* at the beginning of a word. Sometimes it is spelled *x*, as in *xylophone*, or *cz* as in *czar*. On the lines below, write three words that begin with *z*, three words that begin with *x* and three words that begin with *cz*. Use your dictionary for help.

_____

_____

_____

Beginning Vowel Sounds

You have been learning about beginning consonant sounds and the usual ways of spelling them. Vowel sounds are much harder to spell, because there are so many of them and they are spelled in so many ways.

The short vowel sounds are the easiest, because they are almost always spelled the same way. The short a (ă) at the beginning of a word like *add* is spelled *a*; the short e (ĕ) as in *end* is usually spelled *e*; the short o (ŏ) is spelled *o*, and the short u (ŭ) is spelled *u*, except before *v* or *th* when it is spelled with an *o*, as in *oven* and *other*.

The short *i* is most often spelled *i*, except sometimes in an unaccented syllable, when it may be spelled *e*.

1. On each line below, write words that begin with the vowel sound shown at the left side of the line. Use your dictionary to help you find words with the right diacritical mark.

(ă) _____

(ĕ) _____

(ĭ) _____

(ŏ) _____

(ŭ) _____

2. Often the first sound of a word of more than one syllable, when the first syllable is not the accented syllable, sounds like the schwa sound (ə). Any one of the vowels may stand for that sound. If you find that your dictionary marks the first sound differently from the schwa, don't worry about it. It may just be hard for you to hear the difference. In the word *elect*, for example, it may sound like ə lĕkt′ to you, but the phonetic spelling is ĭ lĕkt′. After each phonetic spelling below, write the word.

ə kûr′ _____ ĭ m ăj′ĭn _____ ə round′ _____

ə bout′ _____ ĭ lek′shən _____ əb struct′ _____

əb jĕkt′ _____ ə lōn _____ ə pŏn′ _____

Long Vowel Sound Beginnings

Many words begin with long vowel sounds. Some examples are: able, eager, idle, over.

The long a (ā) sound is most often spelled *a* or *ai* at the beginning of a word. If the word is the number 8 or one of its derivatives, the a is spelled *eigh*.

The long e (ē) at the beginning is most often spelled with e, or ea.

The long i (ī) is most often spelled *i* at the beginning of a word, unless the word is a derivative of *eye*. But there are a few oddball words like *aisle* and *eider* which have a different spelling. You're most likely to find a word that begins with long i beginning with the letter *i*.

Two common spellings of the beginning long o (ō) are *o* and *oa*. A few words begin with *ow*.

1. The words below all begin with the long a (ā) sound. Each one is spelled phonetically. Find the words in your dictionary and write their correct spelling.

āk′ing _____ ā′jənt _____ āl′ment _____

ā′lər ŏn _____ ā′tēn′ _____ ā′lē ən _____

2. The following words begin with the long *e* sound. Using the phonetic spelling, find the correct spelling of each in your dictionary and write it.

ē′vən _____ ē′rē _____ ē′grĕs′ _____

ē′zəl _____ ē′thər _____ ē′gəl _____

3. The words below begin with the long ō sound. Use your dictionary to find the correct spelling and write it after the phonetic spelling of the word.

ō′pən _____ ō′nər shĭp′ _____ ō′shən _____

ōt′mēl _____ ō′vəl _____ ō′ĭng _____

4. In your dictionary, find the correct spelling for each of the following words, all beginning with the long *i* sound. Write the spelling after the phonetic spelling.

ī′təm _____ ī′sīt′ _____ ī′lăsh _____

ī dē′əl _____ ī′dəl īz′ _____ ī′sə lāt _____

Other Vowel Sounds

Some other vowel sounds that you will use in finding out how to spell words correctly are the following:

The *oi* sound is found at the beginning of *oil* and at the end of *boy*. The phonetic spelling is always *oi*, and it is almost always spelled *oi* or *oy*.

The *ou* sound comes at the beginning of *owl* and *out* and at the end of *how* and *now*. The phonetic spelling is *ou* and it almost always is spelled *ou* or *ow*.

The long oo ($\overline{oo}$) sound is one that has many spellings. It may be spelled *oo* as in *boot*, *ou* as in *soup*, *u* as in *rule*, *ew* as in *new*, and *ue* as in *blue*. There are some spellings that are used very seldom, such as the *oe* in *shoe* and the *ough* in *through*.

1. Find the correct spelling for each of the phonetically spelled words that follow. Write the correct spelling on the line after the phonetic spelling.

ois′tər _____   mois′ən _____   jouns _____

al′loi _____   kroud _____   ī′brou′ _____

2. Look up each of the words below. They all end with the $\overline{oo}$ sound. After each word write the homonyms which are given at the end of the definition.

do (d$\overline{oo}$) _____   shoe (sh$\overline{oo}$) _____   new (n$\overline{oo}$) _____

blue (bl$\overline{oo}$) _____   through (thr$\overline{oo}$) _____   flue (fl$\overline{oo}$) _____

3. The y$\overline{oo}$ sound is just like the word *you*. At the beginning of a word, it is most often spelled *u*, but sometimes *eu*. In the middle and at the ends of words, it may be spelled *u*, *ue*, or *ew*. For each phonetically spelled word below, find the correct spelling.

ky$\overline{oo}$t _____   my$\overline{oo}$′zĭk _____   fy$\overline{oo}$ _____

y$\overline{oo}$′nĭt _____   ky$\overline{oo}$′rē əs _____   y$\overline{oo}$′rəp _____

One unusual spelling of the y$\overline{oo}$ sound is found in *beauty* and in derivatives of that word.

Vowels Before r

We mentioned earlier that when a vowel sound is followed by the sound of *r*, it is changed so much that it often has to have a special diacritical mark. The a sound that you hear in the homophones *pare*, *pair*, and *pear*, is marked â. These homophones show you three common ways of spelling that sound. Another spelling is in the prefix *aero-*. Some other spellings you will meet are in the words *where*, and *their*. The sound î, is the one you hear in *cheer*, *fear*, *here*, and *pierce*. Those four words contain the most common spellings of that sound, but you may find a word in which it is spelled *y*.

The ä sound is often heard before *r* as in *arm*, but it is also heard without an *r*, as in *father*, *palm*, and *rah*. It is usually spelled *a* or *ah*, sometimes *al* and once in a great while *ea*.

1. At the left side of each line below is the phonetic spelling of one of the sounds you have just read about. After it are several words containing that sound.

In each word, circle the letter or letters that stand for the sound at the left.

â   wear   aerospace   airplane   fair   preparing   there   their

î   steer   here   dear   fierce   lyric   pier   clear

ä   calm   hurrah   part   garage   heart   start   alarm

2. Another sound that is always heard before an *r* sound is û which you can hear in *her*, *bird*, *fur*, and after the letter *w*, it is spelled *ea* and even *y*. In each word below, circle the letter or letters that stand for the û sound.

firmly   curtain   myrtle   verb   heard   lurk   stir   earth

early   urge   furthest   earn   world   purchase   worthy

3. One sound is spelled in a number of different ways. That is the sound you hear before *r* as in *order*, but it also occurs in words like *all*, *awful*, *autumn*, *often*, and *fourth*.

The ô sound is usually spelled *o* before *r* but sometimes *ou*. It is often spelled *a* before *l*, *aw* and *au* at various times, and after *w* it is most often spelled *a* as in *war*. Two other spellings are *augh* as in *taught* and *ough* as in *thought*.

In each word circle the letter or letters that stand for the ô sound.

fallout   course   paw   warden   pause   daughter   brought

caught   warbler   awkward   stork   flaw   caller   taut

Middle and Final Vowels

So far, we have been discussing mostly beginning vowel sounds and how they are spelled. However, when a vowel sound occurs at the middle or at the end of a word, it may be spelled differently from the way it is at the beginning.

1. The long *a* sound (ā) is most often written *ai* or *a*, but in the middle and at the end of a word, it may be spelled in several different ways. It may be spelled *a* or *ai* as it is at the beginning. In each word below, circle the letter of letters that stand for the long *a* sound. Try to remember these ways of spelling it.

mayor   major   rein   claim   stay   obey   straight   weight

2. At the beginning of a word the long *e* (ē) is usually spelled *e* or *ea*. These spellings are used in the middle of words too, but there are many other spellings. In the words below, circle the letter or letters that stand for ē.

fever   preach   piece   ceiling   beetle   receive   key   only

3. The long *i* (ī) at the beginning of a word is most often spelled *i*, but there are other spellings that are used in the middle and at the end of a word. Circle the letters that stand for ī.

cider   sign   night   eider   aisle   sky   pie   cycle

4. The long *o* (ō) sound is spelled *o* or *oa* most often at the beginning of a word, but other spellings also are used in the middle or at the end. Circle the letters that stand for ō.

rover   boat   bowling   toe   sew   though   below   shoulder

5. The short oo (o͝o) sound that you hear in *foot* and *good* occurs only in the middle of words. It is almost always spelled *oo*, but sometimes *u*, and *ould* as in *would*. Most short vowel sounds are spelled with just the letter itself, as in *add*, *end*, *if*, *on*, and *up*. Sometimes other spellings are used. After each vowel sound below are some words containing that sound. Circle the letter or letters that stand for the sound.

ĕ   end   head   measure   steps   ĭ   myth   with   stick   simple

o͝o   stood   should   woods   put   ŭ   rough   stump   trouble   come

Middle and Final Consonants

Most of the things you learned about initial consonant sounds and their spellings are also true in the middle of words and at the end. However, you often find a consonant doubled, especially after a short vowel as in *baggy*.

Following are some consonant sounds that have various spellings. After each one is a list of words. Circle the letter or letters that stand for the sound.

j   wedge   reject   agent   adjective   cage   badger   wages

s   fussy   malice   descend   geese   mess   center   psalm

ch   much   witch   picture   richer   peach   snatch   watch

z   nose   razor   fuzzy   cheese   rising   misery   amaze

1. The sound that the letter x stands for is phonetically spelled *ks* and it has a variety of spellings. It is never heard at the beginning of a word, but often in the middle or end. Find the *ks* sound in each of these words and circle the letter or letters that stand for it.

accept   succeed   except   taxes   sticks   exercise   exceed   influx

2. The *sh* sound at the beginning and end of words is most often spelled *sh*, but a few words have the *ch* spelling at the beginning and *che* at the end. In the middle of words the *sh* sound has many spellings, the most common being *ci*, as in *special*, *si* as in *mission* and *ti* as in *action*. Another is *ss* as in *pressure*. Circle the letter or letters that stand for the *sh* sound in each word below.

magician   fissure   addition   omission   official   reduction

3. The suffixes and prefixes which you have read about earlier will help you to spell or to find the word in your dictionary. One suffix that it is always wise to look up is the one that is phonetically written ə b əl. You'll find it in words like *washable* and *visible*. There is no easy rule to follow for deciding whether it should be spelled *able* or *ible*. The only safe way to know the correct spelling is to look it up. Look up each word that follows (all ending in ə b əl) and write the correct spelling.

rĭ spek′ tə bəl _____   sen′sə bəl _____

ăk sĕp′ tə bəl _____   pûr mĭs′ə bəl _____

Wrap-Up Page

Find the correct spelling for each phonetically spelled word that follows. Use what you know about possible spellings of both consonant and vowel sounds and what you know about prefixes and suffixes. Notice that the prefixes <u>re</u>, <u>de</u>, and <u>ex</u> are often spelled phonetically as i, when they are unaccented syllables. Read the definition and then write a sentence using the word. If any homophones are given at the end of the definition, write a sentence using each.

rĕj´ĭs trē _____

_____

pān _____

_____

rĭ sĕp´ shən _____

_____

kən vûr tə bəl _____

_____

dī lĭsh´ əs _____

_____

dĭ lĭt´ fəl _____

_____

ôr´ dn ĕr ē _____

_____

ĭm plô´zə bəl _____

_____

UNIT 6
Additional Information

In addition to supplying the pronunciation, meaning and spelling of words that you read and want to use, your dictionary has many other kinds of information.

One kind of information is that about famous people. You won't find as many people listed in your dictionary as you find in an encyclopedia, nor will you find as much about each one. However, after the entry for each famous person who is listed, you'll find the year of his birth and the year of his death and the reason why the person is important.

People are listed alphabetically by their last names. For example, **Wilson, Woodrow** is the listing for **Woodrow Wilson**.

1. After each man's name that follows, write the year of birth and death.

George Washington_____ Thomas Jefferson_____ Benjamin Franklin_____

2. How old was each one when the Declaration of Independence was signed in 1776?

Washington_____ Jefferson_____ Franklin_____

3. Write the years of birth and death of Abraham Lincoln. _____

Was Jefferson still living when Lincoln was born? _____

4. Who was James K. Polk? _____

5. What was the nationality of each person listed below?

Hans Christian Anderson _____   Frederic Chopin _____

William Shakespeare _____   Leonardo da Vinci _____

Paul Revere _____   Louis Pasteur _____

Hernando de Soto _____   Jacques Cartier _____

Henry Hudson _____   William F. Cody _____

6. How many men are listed under the entry **Roosevelt**? _____

7. How many men are listed under the entry **Adams**? _____

75

Names in Geography

In addition to the names of famous people, your dictionary gives names of well-known cities, large rivers, mountains, and countries. It also lists continents and oceans. The population figures are given for cities and countries, as well as for some of the islands listed.

1. Label each of the following *city*, *river*, *mountain*, *island*, or *country*.

Amazon _____   Bali _____

Mont Blanc _____   Volga _____

Istanbul _____   Gambia _____

Bangui _____   Seine _____

Matterhorn _____   Kabul _____

2. Name the country in which each of these cities can be found.

Liverpool _____   Seoul _____

Heidelberg _____   Toronto _____

Ankara _____   La Paz _____

Capetown _____   Cleveland _____

3. What are the populations of these cities or countries?

Paris _____   Bangkok _____   Iran _____

Annapolis _____   Cologne _____   Sacramento _____

South Africa ____   Greece _____   Rangoon _____

Afghanistan _____   London _____   Ethiopia _____

4. Name the capital of each of these states:

Arizona _____   Oregon _____

Connecticut _____   Maine _____

Alaska _____   Louisiana _____

76

How Pictures Help

You know that your dictionary tells you how to pronounce and to spell words, as well as to find their meanings. Another help that your dictionary gives you is to supply pictures of birds, animals, and objects which are hard to describe fully in words and which you may never have seen.

1. On the lines below, write the names of eight animals that are pictured in your dictionary and which you have never seen.

_____   _____

_____   _____

_____   _____

_____   _____

2. Write the names of eight birds pictured in your dictionary— birds that you have never seen.

_____   _____

_____   _____

_____   _____

_____   _____

3. Where would you expect to find:

a crow's-nest? _____

cymbals? _____

a scythe? _____

a lei? _____

a valance? _____

a serape? _____

Language Families

It may surprise you to know that there are families of languages, just as there are families of people. The languages of Europe are all members of a huge family, known as the Indo-European Family.

Of course, there are many different kinds of relatives in a family. The closest relatives are inside your own family, parent, brothers, and sisters. Also there are aunts, uncles, and cousins.

Languages have relatives too. Two big families in the Indo-European group are the Germanic and the Romance. The Romance languages are not called that because they are romantic, but because they are related to the Roman or Latin. The Romance languages are French, Italian, Spanish, and Portuguese. Another family is the Germanic group. That includes German, Swedish, Norwegian, Danish and the old type of English.

1. The Latin or Roman word for *mother* is *mater* (mä târ). Find two words in your dictionary that have the word *mater* and the meaning of *mother* in them.

2. The Latin or Roman word for *father* is *pater*. (pä târ). Find two words in your dictionary that have the word *pater* and the meaning of *father* in them.

3. Who are your *maternal* grandparents?

4. Who are your *paternal* grandparents?

5. The Latin word for *brother* is *frater*. Find two words in your dictionary that have the word *frater* and the meaning of *brother* in them.

6. What two English words contain *aqua*, Latin for *water*?

Kinds of English

The people who really first spoke English were two tribes from what is now Germany, the Angles and the Saxons. Because the island was often raided by people from the Scandinavian countries, the language was mostly German, but with some addition from Danish, Swedish, and Norwegian. This language is called **Old English**.

You would have trouble understanding Old English if you heard it or tried to read it. Old English was spoken and written over nine hundred years ago, and as people speak any language, it gradually changes in sound and sometimes in meanings of some words.

1. The names of our week days come from Old English, some being named for the old Germanic gods.

Which day was named for the sun? _____

Which day was named for the moon? _____

Which day was named for Thor, the god of thunder? _____

Which day was named for Freya, the goddess of beauty? _____

Which day was named for Tiu, the god of war? _____

Which day was named for Woden, the king of Germanic gods? _____

Which day was named for Saturn? _____

2. The names we use for months came from the old Roman gods or from Latin words. After each item listed below, write the name of the month that comes from it.

Mars, the Roman god of war _____

Juno, the queen of the old Roman gods _____

Julius Caesar, a Roman Emperor _____

Augustus Caesar, another Roman Emperor _____

Septem, the Latin word for the number *seven* _____

Octo, the Latin word for the number *eight* _____

Homograph Origins

Old English was a member of the Germanic family. In 1066, the Normans from northern France invaded England and conquered its people. The Normans were the governors and the native English people were ruled by them. The Normans spoke French of those days and the English had to learn some of the language to get along with their new masters. The Normans also learned English and finally the two languages became one, known as **Middle English**.

French, of course, is one of the languages closely tied to Latin, and many of our words came to the English language through the French, though they were originally Latin.

Homographs, you remember, are words that are spelled just the same way, but have different meanings, usually because they started out in different languages. Your dictionary gives word origins in notes on the margins.

1. Find the following groups of homographs in the outside margin. In the first blank after each word, write the language the word comes from. Then write the original word.

Homographs	Original Language	Original Word	Homographs	Original Language	Original Word
excise[1]	_____	_____	flat[1]	_____	_____
excise[2]	_____	_____	flat[2]	_____	_____
reef[1]	_____	_____	noodle[1]	_____	_____
reef[2]	_____	_____	noodle[2]	_____	_____
gill[1]	_____	_____	fine[1]	_____	_____
gill[2]	_____	_____	fine[2]	_____	_____
pitch[1]	_____	_____	hatch[1]	_____	_____
pitch[2]	_____	_____	hatch[2]	_____	_____
boil[1]	_____	_____	like[1]	_____	_____
boil[2]	_____	_____	like[2]	_____	_____

More Word Origins

In addition to giving you the language origins of all groups of homographs, the outside margins have statements about other words and what language they came from, or the word may be illustrated by a picture. Using the outside margins for help, answer the questions that follow.

1. Did the word **hundred** first appear in Old English or Middle English? _____

2. What is the original language for **coleslaw**? _____

   What did that word mean? _____

3. From what Latin word did the word **integer** come? _____

   What did the Latin word really mean? _____

4. From what language did the word **coach** originally come? _____

   What was the spelling of that word in French? _____

5. Is a **clavicle** a bone or a musical instrument? _____

   What is another name for **clavicle**? _____

6. What is the origin of the word **crown**? _____

   What English word starts with the Latin word for **crown**? _____

7. How was **Norway** first spelled in English? _____

   What was the meaning of that name? _____

8. From what language did we get the word **reindeer**? _____

   What American animal is very much like it? _____

9. Are the English **robin** and the American **robin** just alike? _____

   Which one is the larger bird? _____

   Who named the American robin? _____

Science Information

Your dictionary gives a great deal of information on scientific subjects. Some of it is in the definitions, but in the outside margin, you will find additions to what is given in the definitions.

If there is more information given in the outside margin you will find this at the end of the definition: [SEE NOTE]

Use your dictionary to answer the questions that follow. Read both the definitions and the notes in the outside margins.

1. What do these animals have in common: **brontosaurus, eohippus, dodo**?

2. For whom is the **Eustachian tube** named?

3. What four substances did the ancient Greeks consider **elements**?

4. What is the important use of **carbon 14**?

5. Why are **fingerprints** useful in identification?

6. Who would be most concerned with an **apogee**, an astronaut, a pharmacist, or a carpenter?

7. What are some dangerous sources of **carbon monoxide**?

8. Name six of the ten parts of the human **eye**.

9. What parts of a **flower** are labeled in the illustration?

10. What are two uses of the gas **argon**?

Interesting Sidelights

Besides word derivations and scientific information, the notes in the outside margins supply historical information, geographical information and some items that are put in just because they are interesting.

Using your dictionary, especially the material in the outside margins, answer the following questions:

1. Where does the word *sideburns* come from?

2. A bikini is a two-piece bathing suit. Where did it get its name?

3. When was "The Star-Spangled Banner" made our national anthem?

4. When and where was the first large epidemic of influenza?

5. For whom are the Nobel Prizes named? Why is he famous?

6. Who started the expression, the "heebie-jeebies?"

7. How would you write the words Morse Code in Morse Code?

8. Write one quotation about the Constitution of the United States.

9. What rhyme helps you to remember the number of days in each month?

Special Labels

In the definitions of words, you have found labels for parts of speech. Another kind of label tells you what the standing of the word is in speaking and writing nowadays.

One such label is the word *archaic* (är kā′ ik). That means that the word is very old and rarely used, probably from Old English or Middle English. The pronouns *thee* and *thou*, which have been replaced by *you*, are two examples of archaic words.

The label *informal* means that the word is acceptable in conversation or in letters to family and friends, but it is not acceptable in business letters or themes or school reports. Some words are labeled *slang*. This means that the word is not considered standard English, even though it is very colorful. Sometimes slang words stay around and are finally accepted as part of the language, but most slang expressions go out of use relatively soon.

1. In each sentence that follows, one word is archaic. Find that word and draw a line under it. Check the definition, because a word may be archaic in only one meaning.

How doth the little busy bee improve each shining hour!
My country, 'tis of thee, Sweet land of liberty.
Methinks I saw an elf and gnome.

2. Which of these words and phrases are informal? Check each one.

gym _____ fish story _____ hoodlum _____ car _____

funny bone _____ bike _____ copter _____ early bird _____

3. Put a check mark after each word that is labeled *slang*.

mutt _____ bonehead _____ cheapskate _____ egghead _____

blabbermouth _____ gyp _____ hijack _____ eggplant _____

4. Look up these words in your dictionary. After each, write *archaic*, *informal*, or *slang*, as it is labeled.

big shot _____ betwixt _____ dost _____

haywire _____ canst _____ two bits _____

Final Wrap-Up (Unit 1)

This page and the eleven pages that follow will give you a chance to show how well you can use the dictionary, putting into practice all the items you have been learning about in the six units.

Each page tells you from which unit the particular items are taken, so, if you have forgotten, you can always turn back to the unit for help.

1. After each word that follows, write the quarter of the dictionary in which you would look for it.

dismal _____ sorrowful _____ vigil _____

koala _____ lissome _____ panther _____

wallaby _____ zither _____ osprey _____

2. Check each word below that would be found on a page with these guide words: **pleat | plop**. Put an x after each word that would not be found there.

placid _____ plenty _____ plight _____ plod _____ pliers _____

pliable _____ piebald _____ pledge _____ plover _____ please _____

3. Number the words in each list to show the order in which they would come in your dictionary.

_____ marsh   _____ shellac   _____ eglantine   _____ lubricate

_____ Mars   _____ shelf   _____ e.g.   _____ loyalty

_____ marshal   _____ she'll   _____ effusive   _____ lunch

_____ mar   _____ shingle   _____ egg[1]   _____ LP

_____ marshland   _____ shellfish   _____ eggplant   _____ luau

_____ marshy   _____ shelve   _____ egg[2]   _____ loyalist

_____ march   _____ shepherd   _____ egret   _____ lozenge

_____ maritime   _____ shelter   _____ egotism   _____ lox[1]

85

Final Wrap-Up (Unit 2)

These two pages will review the information given in Unit 2 of this activity book. If you find you have forgotten any part of the information, turn back to pages 15 through 29.

Use the pronunciation key given in your dictionary, either the short one given at the bottom of each left-hand page or the complete key which is inside the front cover.

1. Following each word in heavy black type is its pronunciation. Below each one are three words or phrases. Underline the one that most nearly rhymes with the word.

ex·pe·dite ĕk′spĭ dīt′
next is right

leaks a bit

wrecks a mitt

min·u·et mĭn′yo͞o et′
will do it

win a bet

pin you yet

boutique bo͞o tēk′
who is new

you peek

new wreck

cy·clo·tron sī′klə trŏn′
I alone

like a fawn

lick a cone

glad·i·o·lus glăd′ē ō′ləs
made a bonus

Daddy told us

had to fool us

phosphorus fŏs′for əs
close the bus

before us

loss for us

2. Before each sentence below are two or three homophones. Decide which one would make sense in the sentence. Write that homophone in the blank.

(creak, creek) Are there any fish in that little _____?

(stake, steak) How would you like your _____ cooked?

(to, too, two) My last year's coat is now much _____ short for me.

(there, their, they're) Bill and Joe say _____ not coming with us.

(write, rite, right) To get to the library, turn _____ at the corner.

(pale, pail) Jack and Jill went up the hill to fetch a _____ of water.

(steel, steal) These tools are made of stainless _____.

Final Wrap-Up (Unit 2)

3. At the beginning of each line below is a word write a sentence using the word as a verb. in heavy black type. On the line after the word,

brake _____

desire _____

whisper _____

4. On each line, write a sentence using the word in heavy type as a noun.

fall _____

rebel _____

plant _____

5. On each line write a sentence using the word in heavy type as an adjective.

clear _____

perfect _____

ideal _____

6. Following are some homographs. Use each one in a sentence after you check its meaning in your dictionary.

mint[1] _____

mint[2] _____

batter[1] _____

batter[2] _____

pool[1] _____

pool[2] _____

rest[1] _____

rest[2] _____

Final Wrap-Up (Unit 3)

In order to do the exercises on this page, you will need to consult the dictionary definitions.

In the first group, you will find questions. The definitions of the words in heavy black type will help you to answer each question.

In the second group, you should find a synonym for each word in heavy black type. Rewrite the sentence, using the synonym in place of that word.

1. What is another name for the **buttonwood tree**? _____
2. Where would you expect to see a **chevron**? _____
3. Where are **davits** used? _____
4. Is an **earwig** an insect or something to wear? _____
5. If you had a **handbill**, would you read it or eat it? _____
6. Is an **indigent** person wealthy? _____
7. Who would use a **mattock**, a gardener or a carpenter? _____
8. If you had a **nougat**, would you eat it or drink it? _____
9. Could curtains be made of **organdy**? _____
10. How many legs does a **spoonbill** have? _____
11. Captain Kidd was a famous **buccaneer**.

_____

12. I'd like to ride on a **carousel**.

_____

13. Indians used birch bark to **construct** their canoes.

_____

14. I was **perplexed** by his treatment of me.

_____

Final Wrap-Up (Unit 3)

In each sentence below, the word in heavy type is either a homograph or a word that has more than one meaning listed in the dictionary.

If the word is a homograph, write the word with the correct superscript number (pool¹). Otherwise, write *Meaning* and the number of the meaning which is used in that sentence. Use your dictionary, of course.

1. Have you ever seen a **periwinkle** clinging to a rock? _____

2. A **leaf** has been torn out of this book. _____

3. I heard a good **joke**, but I can't remember it. _____

4. Another name for an **ounce** is snow leopard. _____

5. The **camel** is often called the ship of the desert. _____

6. The explorers visited the **crater** of an extinct volcano. _____

For each word below, write a sentence that illustrates just what the word means. Imagine that you are trying to explain it to a much younger child or someone just learning English.

snug _____

relation _____

moat _____

implement _____

jest _____

credible _____

89

Final Wrap-Up (Unit 4)

To do the exercises on these two pages, you will need to remember what you learned about inflective and derived forms of root words, as well as idioms, phrasal verbs and nouns used as modifiers.

If you think you need a review, turn back to Unit 4 which starts on page 45 and check back on the meanings of all the terms used in that unit.

1. Each word that follows may be used as a singular noun. In the space that follows the word, write its plural form. Remember that some nouns form plurals irregularly.

prefix _____   squash _____   child _____

witch _____   woman _____   sheep _____

mouse _____   house _____   goose _____

2. After each adjective below, write the comparative and superlative forms.

big _____   smart _____

snappy _____   flat _____

slow _____   sloppy _____

3. Fill in the spaces in the chart below:

Verb	+ -s or -es	+ -d or -ed	+ -ing
watch			
carry			
omit			

4. Write the word made by each combination of prefix, root, and suffix.

un- + happy + ly _____   re- + fresh + ment _____

re- + cycle + ing _____   un- + work + able _____

dis- + respect + -ful _____   un- + deny + -able _____

Final Wrap-Up (Unit 4)

5. Find an idiom under each of the following words. Use the idiom in a sentence of your own.

cover _____

date _____

hot _____

note _____

private _____

grant _____

6. Find in your dictionary how each of these words may be used as a noun modifier. Write a sentence, using the word as a modifier.

crime _____

game _____

storm _____

practice _____

stationery _____

grammar _____

7. For each entry that follows, find a phrasal verb and use it in a sentence.

double _____

face _____

mix _____

palm _____

sign _____

grow _____

Final Wrap-Up (Unit 5)

When you are trying to find a word and you are not sure how it is spelled, try the ways you know the sounds in that word may be spelled and try each one to find the word.

As you answer the questions on this page, turn back to Unit 5, which begins on page 63 if you need help in remembering what you read about in that unit.

1. If a word begins with the *k* sound and you can't find it under *k*, where else would you look?

   _____

   If the *k* sound is followed by the *w* sound, where would you be likely to find it?

   _____

2. In what ways is the beginning *n* sound spelled? _____

3. In what ways is the beginning *s* sound spelled? _____

4. In what ways may the beginning *j* sound be spelled? _____

5. How may the beginning *sh* sound be spelled? _____

6. In each word below, circle the letter or letters that stand for the long a (ā) sound.

   apron   they   pain   eight   play   great   rein   bouquet

7. In the words below, circle the letter or letters that stand for the long e (ē) sound.

   feel   either   neat   believe   equal   many

8. In the words below, circle the letter or letters that stand for the long i (ī) sound.

   eyelid   icicle   night   pie   try   sign   eider

9. In the words below, circle the letter or letters that stand for the schwa (ə) sound.

   garden   pardon   along   pencil   enough   bogus

10. In the words below, circle the letter or letters that stand for the yōō sound.

    cute   few   beauty   music   feud   eucalyptus   cue

Final Wrap-Up (Unit 5)

Find the correct spelling for each phonetically spelled word below. Use what you know about possible spellings of both consonant and vowel sounds and what you know about prefixes and suffixes. Read the definition of each word and use it in a sentence.

jĕn´ yo͞o ĭn _____

_____

bī´ sĭk əl _____

_____

sĭt´ ĭ zən _____

_____

jăm´ bə rē´ _____

_____

kwŏd´ ro͞o pĕd´ _____

_____

rĕk´ ĭj _____

_____

nŏl´ ĭ jə bəl _____

_____

gĭ tär´ _____

_____

ĕm băr´ əs _____

_____

dĭ zī´ nər _____

_____

Final Wrap-Up (Unit 6)

To do the exercises on this page and the next one, use regular entries in your dictionary and the information given in the outside margins. Sometimes you will need to check with the pictures in the margins as well as the printed notes.

1. Write the answers to these questions:

   a. Were Samuel Adams and George Washington alive at the same time? _____

   b. Who was Walt Whitman? _____

   c. Of what country is Prague the capital? _____

   d. Was Abraham Lincoln or Andrew Johnson our 17th President? _____

   e. Which has the larger population, London or Tokyo? _____

   f. What is the Rhine? _____

   g. Who invented the derringer? _____

   h. Which camel has two humps? _____

   i. Was Leonardo da Vinci alive when Columbus discovered America? _____

   j. What are "flocks" of the following animals called?

   insects _____ lions _____ geese _____ grouse _____

2. You have learned that many words are labeled according to the way they are used in English today. These labels are **status labels**. *Archaic* means *very old*, no longer used in ordinary speech. *Informal* means the word or phrase is all right to use in speech or informal writing. The third label is *slang*.

   After each word or phrase below, write the status label that is given to it in the dictionary.

   betwixt _____

   punk² _____

   know-how _____

   gym _____

   prithee _____

   funny bone _____

94

Final Wrap-Up (Unit 6)

3. Fill in the spaces in the chart below. If two languages are listed, write them both. Write the original word and what it meant. This information is all in the outside margins.

Word	Original Language	Original Word	Meaning of Original
muff²			
gladiolus			
fray²			
elder¹			
diary			
pitcher²			
annual			
April			
skate¹			
stable			
mat¹			
tow¹			
reel¹			

4. Use the pictures and definitions in your dictionary to answer these questions:

   a. How many kinds of prisms are shown in your dictionary? _____

   b. Did a prairie schooner travel on land or on water? _____

   c. Is an English horn used on a car or in an orchestra? _____

   d. How many kinds of compasses are shown in your dictionary? _____

   e. Which has horns, a cheetah or a chamois? _____

   f. For whom was the teddy bear named? _____

   g. How many kinds of birds' nests are pictured in your dictionary? _____

A WORD GAME

1. In the chart below, there are letters in the left hand column. Across the top are categories. Find a word that fits a category and begins with one of the letters at the left. The first one is done for you.

Letters	Liquids	Famous Men	Sports	Clothing	Fruit
L	lemonade				
B					
S					
M					
C					

2. You can use this copy of the chart and make a game of it. Choose any categories and letters that you want to. Just don't use the same letter twice. Now exchange charts with a classmate and see who can fill in the other's chart first.

Letters					